Introducing Zurb Foundation 6

Aravind Shenoy

Apress®

Introducing Zurb Foundation 6

ISBN-13 (pbk): 978-1-4842-1795-5

ISBN-13 (electronic): 978-1-4842-1796-2

Managing Director: Welmoed Spahr
Lead Editor: Louise Corrigan
Development Editor: Jim Markham
Technical Reviewer: Ian Devlin
Editorial Board: Steve Anglin, Pramila Balen, Louise Corrigan, Jim DeWolf,
    Jonathan Gennick, Robert Hutchinson, Celestin Suresh John, Michelle Lowman,
    James Markham, Susan McDermott, Matthew Moodie, Jeffrey Pepper, Douglas Pundick,
    Ben Renow-Clarke, Gwenan Spearing
Coordinating Editor: Jill Balzano
Copy Editor: April Rondeau
Compositor: SPi Global
Indexer: SPi Global
Artist: SPi Global

Distributed to the book trade worldwide by Springer Science+Business Media New York, 233 Spring Street, 6th Floor, New York, NY 10013. Phone 1-800-SPRINGER, fax (201) 348-4505, e-mail orders-ny@springer-sbm.com, or visit www.springeronline.com. Apress Media, LLC is a California LLC and the sole member (owner) is Springer Science + Business Media Finance Inc (SSBM Finance Inc). SSBM Finance Inc is a **Delaware** corporation.

For information on translations, please e-mail rights@apress.com, or visit www.apress.com.

Apress and friends of ED books may be purchased in bulk for academic, corporate, or promotional use. eBook versions and licenses are also available for most titles. For more information, reference our Special Bulk Sales–eBook Licensing web page at www.apress.com/bulk-sales.

Any source code or other supplementary material referenced by the author in this text is available to readers at www.apress.com. For detailed information about how to locate your book's source code, go to www.apress.com/source-code/.

First and foremost, I would like to thank my mother Vatsala for standing beside me throughout my career and while writing this book. She has been my inspiration and motivation. She is my rock, and I dedicate this book to her.

Contents at a Glance

Contents

About the Author

Aravid Shenoy is a senior technical writer by profession. Aravind's core interests are technical and content writing, content development, web design, and business analysis. An engineering graduate from the Manipal Institute of Technology and an author of several books, he is a keen learner and believes that there is always a steep learning curve as life is all about learning.
He was born and raised in Mumbai and resides there. A music buff - he loves listening to Rock n' Roll and Rap. Oasis, R.E.M, The Doors, Dire Straits, Coldplay, Jimi Hendrix and Michael Jackson rule his playlists. He is a firm believer in the quote "Do one thing and do it very well indeed" and in his own words "The most important thing is to be happy."

About the Technical Reviewer

Ian Devlin is interested in all things web, and currently works as a frontend engineer for trivago, in Düsseldorf, Germany. He is an HTML5 Doctor and a founding contributor to Intel's HTML5 Hub and has written articles for a number of online developer zones such as Mozilla, Opera, Intel, and Adobe, and for net magazine. He has also written a book on HTML5 Multimedia and has been technical reviewer for a number of Apress books.

Acknowledgments

In addition to my mother, I also thank my father Gopalkrishna Shenoy, uncle Satish Rao, my aunt Godavari, and my sister Aruna for always making me smile in any situation. I would also like to thank my niece Ajnya who is the echo of my heart and my cousin Ashwin who has always been a pillar of support.

Introduction

As the title suggests this is an introduction to Zurb written for Foundation 6. Zurb has become a useful technology for building fast, responsive websites. Foundation 6 is a powerful CSS framework for developing scalable front-end code fast. Foundation adheres to the mobile-first paradigm and comes with built-in HTML, CSS, and JavaScript plug-ins for creating responsive websites. As the world turns more and more to the use of cell phones as the primary device for browsing the web, it is critical that all sites enable the responsive technologies that make mobile the first priority. The beauty of Zurb is that it saves you the pain of having to develop all of the tools you need to create a responsive website. This book is meant to introduce you to the basic technologies so that you can utilize Zurb, saving you and the end users time and aggravation.

This book provides the basics you need to use Zurb effectively. These include tips on installation, how to use Foundation's new grid system, its layout, content and other features. The book shows you how to include features like typography, utility classes, media, forms, and buttons. There are two chapters dedicated to using the built-in CSS and JavaScript components. For those looking to take the site a bit further from the mainstream CSS results, there is a chapter devoted to Foundation with Sass. This chapter walks you through an example illustrating how to use this CSS pre-processor to make your site a bit more unique. In all, we hope that you will find this a useful and quick read that will get you started with creating responsive and efficient web sites.

Programming Code

The programming code for the examples in this book are located in a zip file that may be updated from time to time. This file may be found in the Source Code/Errata tab on the book's page at Apress.com/9781484217955.

CHAPTER 1

■ ■ ■

Quick Start with Foundation

Foundation is a powerful and intuitive CSS framework created by the folks at Zurb for use in developing front-end code in a quick and efficient manner. Foundation adheres to the mobile-first paradigm and comes with built-in HTML, CSS, and JavaScript plug-ins for creating responsive websites.

Backed by a vibrant community, Foundation is a robust toolkit that helps you create feature-rich websites in a jiffy. Before we delve into it, however, let's first understand why responsive web design is important and what the benefits are of using a *CSS* framework in web design.

Responsive Web Design and CSS Frameworks

Responsive web design is now the norm, given the reach of smartphones and tablets in this digital era. Studies suggest that with the advent of e-commerce, consumers would prefer to purchase from their mobile phones rather than from conventional desktops. Consumers want mobile websites that are fully functional rather than a watered-down version of their bulky desktop counterparts.

Responsive web design adopts a one-site-fits-all approach wherein your website is not limited to a certain device type or screen size. It means that your website will have the same URL and a single code base on all devices, thereby eliminating the need to create separate websites for the mobile and desktop versions. This device-agnostic strategy also results in easy code handling and maintenance. Google recommends responsive web design as an industry-wide best practice. The most important aspect of responsive web design is creating an optimal user experience, as users will have access to the same content irrespective of the device. You do not have to worry about future scalability, because responsive websites are fluid in nature.

Writing HTML, CSS, and JavaScript code from scratch for a responsive website can be quite tedious. Add cross-browser compatibility to it and you have an enormous task at hand. Deadlines for the completion of work and the need to maintain consistency in coding among the team of designers make it even more difficult. It can be quite an arduous task indeed to construct the layout and then write loads of JavaScript code to develop a fancy website.

To counter these issues, it is important to have a toolkit that takes into consideration all the constraints involved when designing a feature-rich website. In short, a CSS framework helps you streamline your web-design process and helps you develop a website in an easier and faster way. CSS frameworks come with pre-defined sets of code and utilities that you can use, eliminating worries about the presentation code and freeing you to focus on the imperative tasks in your projects.

A CSS framework not only speeds up development but also takes care of concerns such as cross-browser compatibility and responsiveness. In addition to not writing the code from scratch, you can also reuse the code several times in your projects. A CSS framework supports the Dry principle that states that "every piece of knowledge must have a single, unambiguous, authoritative representation within a system." It means that instead of copy-pasting code at various places in your file, you can create components that can be used wherever necessary.

Enter Foundation: an easy-to-use, potent, and advanced CSS framework that helps you create clean and symmetrical grid-based layouts, thus taking the guesswork out and saving you huge chunks of development time while at the same time ensuring that your website scales effectively over devices of any make or screen size.

Getting Started with Foundation 6

Foundation's usability and semantics-prone pattern makes it the go-to-framework for your web-design projects. In this section, we will look at the process of setting up the Foundation files, which can be downloaded from the main website. You need to go to http://foundation.zurb.com/, where you can see the Foundation homepage, as displayed in Figure 1-1.

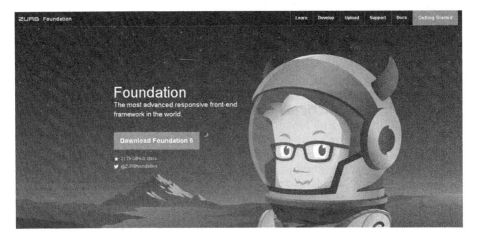

Figure 1-1. *Foundation 6 homepage*

We have used Google Chrome as the browser for code examples in this book; alternatively, you can use Firefox or any compatible browser of your choice. Just make sure that you use the latest version of your browser, as older versions may not support all features.

Refer to the following link to be in sync with information related to browser compatibility:

`http://foundation.zurb.com/sites/docs/compatibility.html`

In the preceding screenshot, you can see the Zurb Foundation homepage. If you decrease the browser size or minimize it, you will see that the site is responsive, meaning it adjusts the layout on screen according to the size of the browser.

See Figure 1-2.

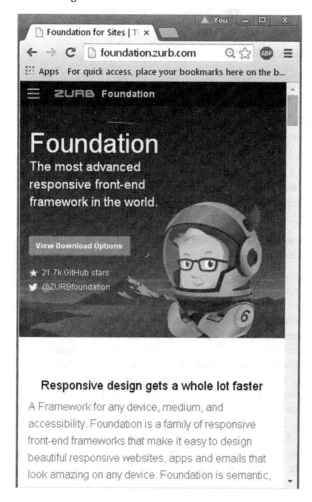

Figure 1-2. Foundation homepage on a small screen

From the preceding screenshot, you can see that the Foundation site is itself responsive.

If you click on the Navicon (also known as the Hamburger icon), you can view the same menu items as are displayed in the top menu bar on both large and medium screens.

On clicking the Download item, you see the four download options available in Foundation, namely *Complete, Essential, Custom,* and *Sass* (see Figure 1-3).

Figure 1-3. Download options in Foundation 6

- The *Complete* version contains all the components and utilities available in Foundation 6.

- The *Essentials* version is a stripped-down version containing the minimum required components, such as Typography, Grid, and buttons without the bloat or clutter.

- The *Custom* version includes only those utilities that you need. You can choose which features you want for your web design and omit the unnecessary ones, thereby reducing the file size considerably.

- The fourth is the *Sass* version, which is used if you want to set your variables and mixins in SCSS.

You need to choose the appropriate version as per your requirements. However, remember that you will have to include all the missing JavaScript and CSS files (along with having to recompile Sass files to CSS if you are using Sass) if you upgrade from a Custom or Essentials download to the comprehensive Complete bundled package.

In our case, we will download the Complete build (i.e., Foundation 6 for Sites).

The advantage of using the Complete version is that you have all the components you could possibly need, meaning you need not include separate files for individual functionality. In real-time scenarios, you can use a custom build, as it will be lightweight and therefore will ensure optimal page-load times. For example, if you only want to use the grid-layout functionality in Foundation, there is no need to include the JavaScript plug-ins. This results in less bloat and clutter in your web design.

Downloading the Complete build will result in a Foundation ZIP file that you can extract and store in the root directory of your useful web projects.

Upon extraction, you will see the following folders and files, as displayed in Figure 1-4.

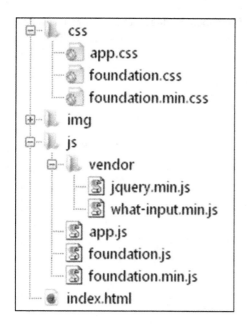

Figure 1-4. *File structure of Foundation 6*

The CSS folder (css) contains all the CSS styles used in Foundation 6. As you can see, you can either use the minified version (foundation.min.css) or the uncompressed version (foundation.css). Also, all your custom stylesheets should be placed in this folder, as it is systematic and helps you avoid confusion (though it is not mandatory).

Note According to semantics, Markup should be separate from Presentation. Hence, it is recommended to not use inline CSS. It is preferable that you keep a separate stylesheet for your presentation. Hence, you are implementing best practices if you keep your stylesheet separately. Similarly, custom stylesheets in Foundation need to be stored in the CSS folder. You can store them anywhere, but keeping all your stylesheets in the CSS folder results in easy code handling and maintenance.

The js folder contains all the pre-defined JavaScript files. You can also place your external JavaScript files in this folder.

The img folder is where you place all the images for your web project.

Finally, we come to the index.html file. If you open this file in a browser, you will see the output depicted in Figure 1-5.

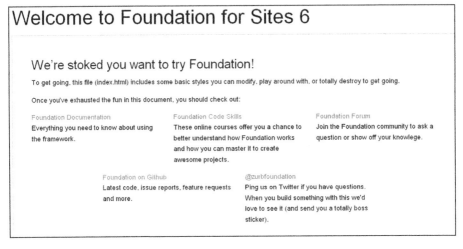

Figure 1-5. Foundation's index.html page

Another way to include Foundation in your web projects is by using the *CDN* (Content Delivery Network).

For starters, a CDN holds copies of your file in several locations across multiple servers. The files can be images, fonts, scripts, and videos.

The advantages of using a CDN for your projects are as follows:

- More servers and easy maintenance

- More bandwidth

- High performance

- Redundancy for fail-safe protection

- Optimized caching settings

- Parallelized downloads

For Foundation, you can find the CDN links on the following webpage (see Figure 1-6):

```
http://cdnjs.com/libraries/foundation
```

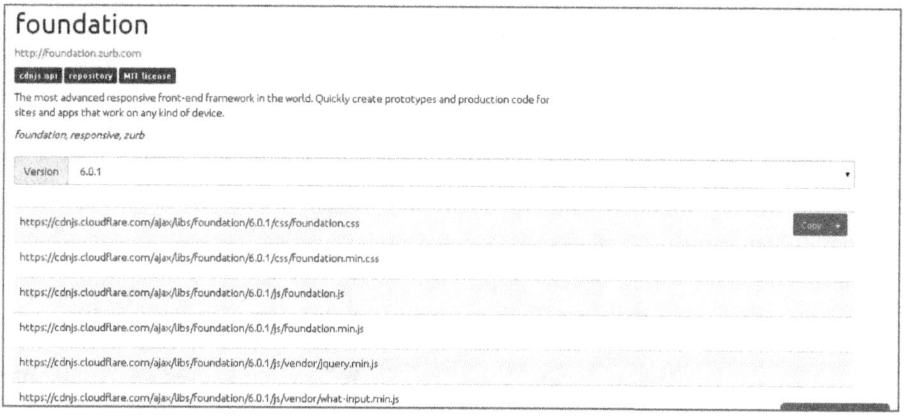

Figure 1-6. *Various CDN links for Foundation*

Instead of using a comprehensive foundation.js CDN, you can opt for a minified version. Similarly, you can use the minified CSS CDN link instead of the regular one. You can also use the jQuery CDN link. We will be discussing the basic markup in Chapter 2.

Remember that you should always be connected to the Internet for CDN, as it is hosted over the web.

We will be using the CDN version links for our code examples throughout the entire book.

▪ **Note** *Foundation 6* is a complete overhaul of its earlier versions (you need not know about the earlier versions of this book, however) and helps you go from prototyping to production with simpler and more lightweight CSS styles, as well as with greater accessibility.

Summary

In this chapter, we took a look at an overview of the Foundation framework. We also gained an understanding of the need for responsive web design and the importance of a CSS framework for web-design projects. We moved on to understanding the different download options for Foundation, where you can choose the build type based on your requirements. In the next chapter, we will look at the symmetrical and clean grid layout that Foundation provides, along with the built-in utility classes.

CHAPTER 2

Grid System and Utility Classes

Foundation is one of the frameworks that adheres to the mobile-first approach. In the earlier days, designers used the traditional approach wherein you built a website for desktops or larger screens initially and then worked them into a watered-down version for mobile devices. Such an approach was tedious—even more so when you tried to create an intuitive and feature-rich website. Add code readability and maintenance to it, and you had a big task on your hands.

However, the mobile-first paradigm advocates designing for smaller screens and then adding content and additional features for the desktop platform. Moreover, with e-commerce, exponentially-increasing bandwidth, and awesome processing power, the mobile revolution has come a long way, as mobile has become the primary avenue for Internet use. Mobile-first design also results in better semantics and advocates an enhanced user experience. Studies have suggested that optimal user experience combined with responsive and adaptive design boosts the SEO rankings for the site significantly.

With Foundation, we have a 12-column grid with the option of adhering to a fixed layout. There is also a new feature called Flexbox grid, which is essentially a float grid with attributes such as automatic sizing, responsive adjustments, alignment, and new source ordering, which is quite handy when it comes to developing intricate websites. Flexbox is available only with Sass; there is no CSS version of it as of now.

In this chapter, you will learn about Foundation's basic markup as well as its grid layout and other attributes, such as centering, offsets, and the nesting of columns. We will also take a look at the various Utility classes.

We will be using Notepad++ for all the examples in this book. Also, we will be using CDN links instead of local CSS, JavaScript, and jQuery files (present in the Foundation package) for examples in this book so as to simulate a real-time scenario.

Set the Base Correctly with Foundation

The HTML markup for a Foundation page is shown in Listing 2-1.

Listing 2-1.

```
<!doctype html>
<html class="no-js" lang="en">
  <head>
    <meta charset="utf-8" />
    <meta name="viewport" content="width=device-width, initial-scale=1.0" />
    <title>Foundation | Interchange</title>
<link rel="stylesheet" href="https://cdnjs.cloudflare.com/ajax/libs/
foundation/6.0.1/css/foundation.min.css">

<script src="https://cdnjs.cloudflare.com/ajax/libs/foundation/6.0.1/js/
vendor/jquery.min.js"></script>
<script src="https://cdnjs.cloudflare.com/ajax/libs/foundation/6.0.1/js/
foundation.min.js"></script>

  </head>
  <body >
  <script src="https://cdnjs.cloudflare.com/ajax/libs/foundation/6.0.1/js/
  vendor/what-input.min.js"></script>
  <script>
      $(document).foundation();
  </script>

  </body>
</html>
```

In Listing 2-1, you can see various tags in the <head> and <body> sections.

Let's look at the <head> section first. In the <head> section, the charset *meta* tag is used to define an *HTML* document's character set. The viewport meta tag helps designers control the *viewport,* which is the portion of the web page visible to the user. While width=device-width sets the width of the page as per the device screen, initial-scale=1.0 instructs the device to display the page without any zooming. Then, we introduce the CDN links. The Foundation CDN links can be found on the following site:

https://cdnjs.com/libraries/foundation

We define the foundation.min.css CDN link in the <link> tag, and this is used for the default CSS file. The jquery.min.js and foundation.min.js links are defined in separate <script> tags. The jquery.min.js link has to be inserted before the foundation.min.js link, as Foundation's JavaScript plug-ins and attributes are dependent on jQuery.

Just before we call the Foundation function, we need to include the what-input.min.js CDN link. This file is used to track the current input method, whether it be a mouse, keyboard, or touchscreen. It helps during scripting interactions, where it exposes a simple API and improves track focus by adding data attributes to the body instead of cluttering the DOM with classes on the elements that can be interacted with.

For more info on what-input, check the following link:

```
https://github.com/ten1seven/what-input
```

Just before closing <body> tag, we call the Foundation function to initialize Foundation's built-in JavaScript plug-ins on your page.

This basic structure will be followed for most of the code samples in this book.

Understanding the Grid Layout

A *grid* layout helps you achieve good readability, high flexibility, and page cohesiveness. By default, you can create powerful and potent layouts with a 12-column Foundation grid. Moreover, you can use attributes such as nesting within the columns, offsets, push-and-pull attributes, and the centering of the grid columns to build aesthetically pleasing websites. The 12-column grid helps you lay out your content in an organized manner.

Before we venture into understanding the grid-layout functionality in Foundation 6, let's look at some common terminology:

> *row* - a horizontal container that spans the width of the web page (or the container width, if it is a nested row)
>
> *column* - vertical columns within a row; you can specify their width using classes
>
> *small* – classes meant for small screens (screens less than 640px in width). For example, if you assign a .small-7 class to an element, that element will span across 7 virtual columns on your mobile screen.
>
> *medium* – classes meant for medium-sized screens such as tablets (to be precise, for screens more than 640px and less than 1024px in width). If you assign a .medium-7 class to an element, that element will span across 7 columns on your tablet screen.
>
> *large* – classes meant for large screens such as desktops and laptops (to be precise, for screens more than 1024 px in width). If you assign a .large-7 class to an element, that element will span across 7 columns on your desktop or laptop screen.

By default, if you specify the small class only and do not mention the medium or large classes, then the larger devices will inherit the styles from the small class. On the other hand, if you just mention the large class and no other responsive size, all the elements will stack on top of each other on a small-screen device.

You can use the small, medium, and large classes together in conjunction if you want to specify the custom width for an element on small-, medium-, and large-screen devices respectively. In the following sections, we will learn about each attribute related to the grid system in Foundation.

Responsiveness in Foundation

You do not have to write separate code for responsiveness when you are using Foundation. Let's understand it by means of an example.

The first thing to be done is to create a row:

```
<div class="row">
  </div>
```

We use the .large classes for larger devices such as desktops and laptops. As mentioned earlier, if we do not use any other responsive class other than the large class, all the columns will stack on top of each other when we reduce the browser size to simulate a mobile screen. The Foundation grid contains 12 columns, and therefore if you want your element to span across the first four columns on a large screen, you need to use the .large-4 class. (But remember, if you define a .small class only, then the larger devices will inherit those styles.)

The code snippet would be as follows:

```
<div class="large-4 columns">
        <h1>Welcome to Foundation</h1>
  </div>
```

If you see the code, you can observe that we have used the word *columns* next to the .large-4 class. It is important to understand that the .columns class is compulsory, as you are defining the span of your element across the 12 virtual columns. You can also use the .column class instead of .columns, as the protocol is the same whether you use the singular or plural verbiage.

We will be using code snippets for the example in the book. For the entire code, you can refer to the code bundle.

In the code examples in this book, we have used sample text from the following link:

```
http://www.catipsum.com/
```

This text is used as sample text and therefore, in the examples, we will use the first three words—i.e., Cat Ipsum dolor...—instead of the entire sample text. However, in the code bundle, you can see the entire text used for that example.

The code snippet shown in Listing 2-2 sheds more light on the grid layout:

Listing 2-2.

```
<div class="row">
        <div class="large-4 columns" style="background: #00FF00;">
              Cat ipsum dolor...
        </div>
        <div class="large-6 columns" style="background: #D2B48C;">
              Cat ipsum dolor...
        </div>
        <div class="large-2 columns" style="background: #FFFF00;">
              Cat ipsum dolor...
        </div>
</div>
```

The output of the code is shown in Figure 2-1.

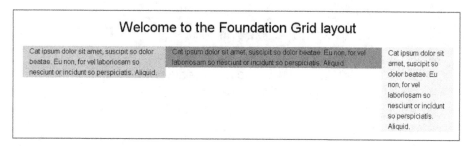

Figure 2-1. Grid functionality

In the code, we used `.large-4`, `.large-6`, and `.large-2` classes for the `<div>` elements with the same text content, and we applied lime, tan, and yellow backgrounds to them respectively. Figure 2-1 shows the way the output looks on a large screen. If you reduce the browser size, the columns will stack on top of each other, as displayed in Figure 2-2.

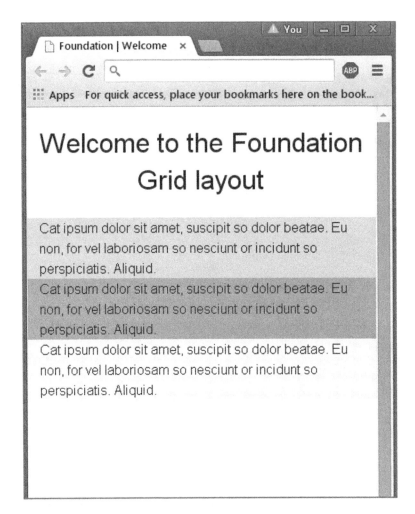

Figure 2-2. *Responsiveness using Foundation*

From the preceding screenshot (Figure 2-2), you can see that the content was adjusted dynamically. When we reduced the browser size, the content was displayed differently without your having to write separate code. Therefore, there is a change in the layout of the web page depending on the user's screen size without your specifically writing custom code for that purpose; responsiveness is baked into the framework.

Adding Custom Width for the Small and Large Screen Resolutions

Foundation was one of the first frameworks to adopt a mobile-first approach. Hence, you can code for small screens and then customize the column size for large screens.

Let's make some changes to the first <div> element in Listing 2-2 by adding a .small-6 class in conjunction with the existing .large-4 class. Do not add the .small-6 class to the remaining <div> elements so that you can see the difference on a small screen.

```
<div class="small-6 large-4 columns" style="background: #00FF00;">
      Cat ipsum text...
  </div>
```

The output of this code is displayed in Figure 2-3.

Figure 2-3. *Grid layout after adding custom width for smaller screens*

As seen in the preceding screenshot, the content spans across six columns on a smaller screen, as we had used the .small-6 class in conjunction with the .large-4 class. Therefore, on a small screen, the content will be spread across six virtual columns, whereas on the large screen, it will span across four virtual columns.

Remember, if you use only the .small class and do not define any other responsive class (i.e., large or medium), then those styles would be adapted for the larger devices. For example, if we had used .small-6 as the only defined class, then the default class for the .large and .medium classes would automatically be .large-6 and .medium-6 respectively.

Nested Columns

Nesting grids is incredibly easy to do in Foundation 6. You can create columns within a defined column by introducing a row inside that defined column.

Let's understand this using a code sample. Create two elements than span across 8 and 4 columns on the 12-column grid respectively (they should contain the text *Parent Column 1* and *Parent Column 2*). Introduce a row inside the element defined by the .small-8 class. We will create two columns (*Nested 1* and *Nested 2*) with widths spanning 8 columns and 4 columns respectively. Then we will introduce a row inside the Nested 1 column and create two columns (with the text Sub-Child1 and Sub-Child 2) using the .small-6 class.

We have used the border CSS property for more clarity in the output. The code snippet used in the example is as displayed in Listing 2-3.

Listing 2-3.

```
<div class="row">
  <div class="small-8 columns" style="border: 5px solid #FF0000">Parent Column 1
    <div class="row">
      <div class="small-8 columns"style="border: 5px solid #7CFC00;">Nested 1
        <div class="row">
          <div class="small-6 columns" style="border: 5px solid
          #0000CD;">Sub Child 1</div>
          <div class="small-6 columns" style="border: 5px solid
          #FF00FF;">Sub Child 2</div>
        </div>
      </div>
      <div class="small-4 columns" style="border: 5px solid #000000;">
      Nested 2</div>
    </div>
  </div>
  <div class="small-4 columns"style="border: 5px solid #228B22;"> Parent Column 2</div>
</div>
 </div>
```

The output of the code would be as displayed in Figure 2-4.

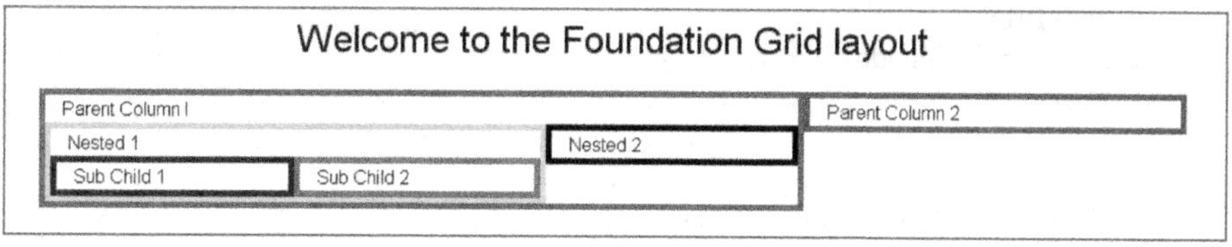

Figure 2-4. Nested grids

The columns (*Nested 1* and *Nested 2*) that were nested inside Parent Column 1 do not occupy the entire grid, but only span the width of the parent column, even though they have been assigned the .small-8 and .small-4 classes. Similarly, the two child columns (*Sub Child 1* and *Sub Child 2*) occupy and fit themselves within their parent column (i.e., Nested 1). Therefore, the child columns occupy the space of their parent columns only and not the entire grid.

Offsets

Offsets in Foundation help you move the columns to the right, meaning you can push columns over for more spacing. Let's understand this using a simple code example. We will create an element spanning two columns on the grid. The next element, spanning four columns across the grid, must be placed to the extreme right.

In order to do so, we will use the .small-2 class for the first column element and .small-4 small-offset-6 class for the second element. The first column element will then occupy the width of two grid columns, and the second column element will occupy four grid columns but will be shifted six columns to the right, as the .offset class shifts the element to the right, as defined in the code.

You also have the .small-centered class, which is used for positioning the column element appropriately in the middle of the screen irrespective of its width across grid columns. In this example, we will use the .small-centered class for positioning the heading inside the header <h1> tags. We have used the inline CSS border property for better illustration.

The code snippet for the Offset property is displayed in Listing 2-4.

Listing 2-4.

```
<body>
 <h1 class="small-2 small-centered columns" style="border: 5px solid
 #228B22;"> Foundation <h1/>
 <div class="row">
  <div class="small-2 columns" style="border: 5px solid #FF0000"> Typical </div>
  <div class="small-4 small-offset-6 columns" style="border: 5px solid
  #FF00FF"> Offset example </div>
 </div>
```

17

```
    <script>
    $(document).foundation();
    </script>
</body>
```

The output of the code is displayed in Figure 2-5.

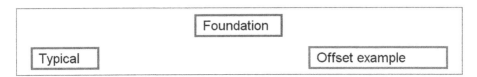

Figure 2-5. *Offsets and centered class*

You can see how offsets and centering work in Foundation 6.

Block Grids

Block grids are a handy feature in Foundation, as they help you evenly split the contents of a list within the grid. You can further customize it for medium or large screens, thereby enhancing the user experience significantly.

The code snippet for the block-grid functionality is displayed in Listing 2-5.

Listing 2-5.

```
<div class="row small-up-3 medium-up-4 large-up-5">
  <div class="column">
    <img src="http://lorempixel.com/image_output/animals-q-c-640-480-8.jpg"
    alt="Animal">
  </div>
  <div class="column">
    <img src="http://lorempixel.com/image_output/nature-q-c-640-480-2.jpg"
    alt="Nature">
  </div>
  <div class="column">
    <img src="http://lorempixel.com/image_output/transport-q-c-640-480-6.
    jpg" alt="Train">
  </div>
   <div class="column">
    <img src="http://lorempixel.com/image_output/city-q-c-640-480-4.jpg"
    alt="City">
  </div>
   <div class="column">
    <img src="http://lorempixel.com/image_output/technics-q-c-640-480-5.jpg"
    alt="Ear Phones">
  </div>
 </div>
```

The output of the code is displayed in Figure 2-6.

In the code snippet in Listing 2-5, we used the following line of code, which explains how the output will be displayed on the large, medium, and small screens:

```
<div class="row small-up-3 medium-up-4 large-up-5">
```

On a large screen, the block grid will contain five images in a single row. On a medium-sized screen, the block grid will contain four images, whereas on a small-screen device, the block grid will contain a maximum of three images in a single row.

Refer to Figure 2-6 to see the output on a large screen.

Figure 2-6. *Block grid on large screen*

Refer to Figure 2-7 to see the output on a medium screen.

Figure 2-7. *Block grid on a medium screen*

Refer to Figure 2-8 to see the output on a small screen.

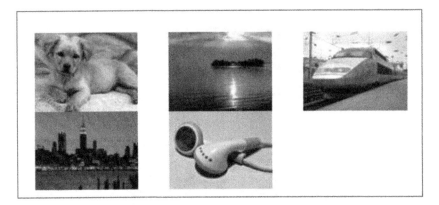

Figure 2-8. *Block grid on a small screen*

You can see the large screen contains five images in a single row while the medium screen will display up to four images in a single row; the small screen will display up to three images in a single row.

For the images, we have used the Lorem-Pixel placeholder facility, which is quite handy, especially when you need images for demonstrating mock-ups. More information about this image and text placeholding website can be found at `http://lorempixel.com/`.

Visibility Classes

Visibility classes are used to hide or show elements based on your device's display size. Let's look at the code snippet displayed in Listing 2-6 to understand them better.

Listing 2-6.

```
<p class="show-for-small-only"><strong> Web Design</strong> </p>
<p class="show-for-medium-only"> <strong> Servers </strong> </p>
<p class="show-for-large"> <strong> Networks </strong> </p>
```

The `.show-for-small-only` class is used when the content needs to be visible only on the small screen, meaning you will not be able to see the content on medium or large screens. The `.show-for-medium-only` class is used when the content needs to be visible on medium screens only. If you want to show content on both medium screens and screens above that size, use the `.show-for-medium` class without the word *only*. Similarly, in the code snippet we have used the `.show-for-large` class, which means the content will be visible on large and extra-large screens.

The output of the code on a large screen will be as displayed in Figure 2-9.

Networks

Figure 2-9. *Content on large and extra-large screens*

In Figure 2-9, you can see that the content can be seen on large screens and above. Refer to Figure 2-10 to view the content as seen on medium screens.

Servers

Figure 2-10. *Content on medium screens*

You can see the content only on the medium screen, as we used the .show-for-medium-only class.

Refer to Figure 2-11 to view the content as seen on a small screen.

Figure 2-11. *Content on small screens only*

We can see the content on small screens only, as we used the .show-for-small-only class.

You can also use .show-for-landscape or .show-for-portrait, depending on whether it is in landscape or portrait orientation.

You can also control what content should disappear depending on device resolution using the .hide visibility classes. Refer to the code bundle to see the code example using the .hide classes.

Utility Classes

Utility classes are helpers that impact the styling of elements in the markup without using the CSS style sheets. Since utility classes are directly involved with the markup, they speed up your work significantly. They can be reused, and they maintain consistency in your code. Let's look at some types of utility classes.

Float Classes

Float classes help you define the float behavior of elements by adding either the .float-left or .float-right class to the elements. You can clear the floats by using the .clearfix class. This class is generally utilized for stacking elements horizontally.

Let's create a callout panel and define the size as well as the float classes along with using the .clearfix class, as displayed in Listing 2-7.

Listing 2-7.

```
<div class="small-10 columns">
 <div class="callout primary clearfix">
  <a class=" alert button float-left">Warning</a>
  <a class="success button float-right">Eureka</a>
 </div>
</div>
```

In Listing 2-7, we have used the .clearfix class for the callout and then created two buttons: a button with an alert class, resulting in a red button, and a button with the .success class, resulting in a green button (Figure 2-12).

Figure 2-12. *Float classes*

In Figure 2-12, you can see the floating behavior using the classes as defined in the code.

Text-Align Classes

You can align the text to the right or left using the text-align classes. You can add more flexibility by adding the size and media query (only). At the basic level, you use the `.text-left`, `.text-right`, `.text-center`, and `.text-justify` classes. However, you can specify the alignment of the text based on the screen size or device orientation by using breakpoints.

Let's look at Listing 2-8.

Listing 2-8.

```
<div class="callout">
 <p class="large-text-right">Cat ipsum dolor sit amet, tempora and error
 explicabo. Aliqua quia ipsam yet rem. </p>
 <p class="large-text-center">Cat ipsum dolor sit amet, tempora and error
 explicabo. Aliqua quia ipsam yet rem.</p>
 <p class="large-text-justify">Cat ipsum dolor sit amet, tempora and error
 explicabo. Aliqua quia ipsam yet rem. </p>
</div>
```

What we have done is create a callout and three paragraphs and used `.large-text-right`, `.large-text-center`, and `.large-text-justify` for the first, second, and third paragraphs respectively.

The output of the code upon execution on a small or medium screen is displayed in Figure 2-13:

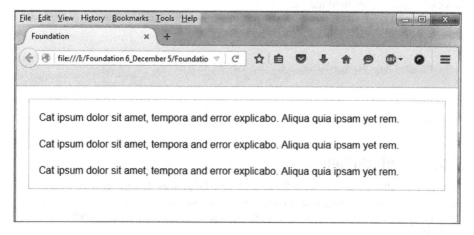

Figure 2-13. Content on small and medium screens

In Figure 2-13, you can see the content aligned in the usual way, as we did not use the alignment classes for the small and medium screens. However, since we used the .large class in conjunction with the text-alignment classes, the output on a large screen will display the alignment as defined in the code.

Refer to Figure 2-14 to understand it better.

Figure 2-14. *Text alignment on a large screen*

In Figure 2-14, you can see the text is aligned to the right, center, and in justified position as per the alignment classes used in the code sample.

To display code examples on an HTML page, Foundation 6 brings in the <code> tag, which will result in output that looks like a code snippet on the webpage.

In Listing 2-9, you can see that we have defined the part that should be displayed as code within the <code> tags. Also, to display the opening and closing tags, we use the < and > Unicode variants.

Listing 2-9.

```
<div class="row">
  <div class="small-10 columns">  <code>&lt;div&gt;</code>Hey you, Music's
  over, Turn off the lights<code>&lt;/div&gt;</code> </div>
</div>
```

Therefore, the output seen in Figure 2-15 displays the code defined between the <code> tags in a highlighted manner.

 Hey you, Music's over, Turn off the lights

Figure 2-15. *Code tags*

Right-to-Left Support

Foundation 6 allows you the flexibility to work with languages that are read from right to left, such as Hebrew, Arabic, and Japanese, to mention a few.

Consider the Listing 2-10 code snippet in English, which is in the usual left-to-right direction:

Listing 2-10.

```
<div class="callout secondary">

<p>Cat ipsum dolor sit amet, tempora and error explicabo. Aliqua quia ipsam
yet rem. Doloremque rem. Inventore. Corporis eius. Totam illo aspernatur yet
amet. Eaque quaerat pariatur. Ipsam ex so pariatur yet laudantium but ipsa
but aute lorem. Deserunt eaque adipisci. Aut nisi yet nostrum quia illo ad.
Ullam ullamco. Minim magna exercitationem for consectetur. </p>

<p>Cat ipsum dolor sit amet, tempora and error explicabo. Aliqua quia ipsam
yet rem. Doloremque rem. Inventore. Corporis eius. Totam illo aspernatur yet
amet. Eaque quaerat pariatur. Ipsam ex so pariatur yet laudantium but ipsa
but aute lorem. Deserunt eaque adipisci. Aut nisi yet nostrum quia illo ad.
Ullam ullamco. Minim magna exercitationem for consectetur. </p>

<p>Cat ipsum dolor sit amet, tempora and error explicabo. Aliqua quia ipsam
yet rem. Doloremque rem. Inventore. Corporis eius. Totam illo aspernatur yet
amet. Eaque quaerat pariatur. Ipsam ex so pariatur yet laudantium but ipsa
but aute lorem. Deserunt eaque adipisci. Aut nisi yet nostrum quia illo ad.
Ullam ullamco. Minim magna exercitationem for consectetur. </p>

</div>
```

Suppose we were to use the right-to-left direction; all you need to do is add the direction for the RTL feature tag, as defined in the <html> tag:

```
<html class="no-js" dir="rtl">
```

Upon execution of the code, you will see that the content is shifted to the right of the screen, as shown in Figure 2-16, which depicts the right-to-left placement.

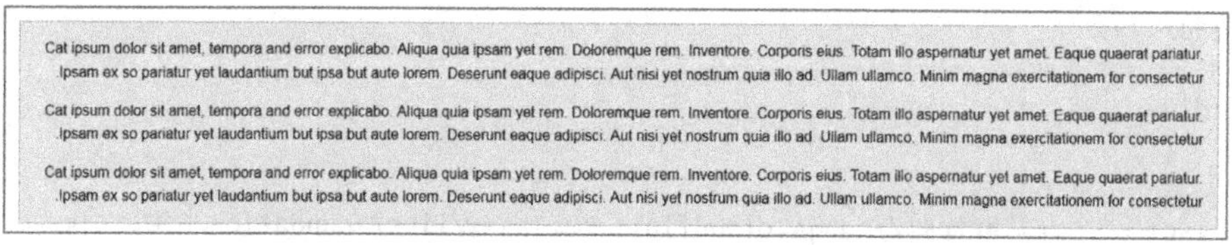

Figure 2-16. *RTL direction*

You can also use the language attribute specific to the language being used on the web page. In the <html> tag, you need to use the lang attribute and give it the value as defined for that language in Foundation.

Suppose we were to use the Japanese language. You can define it in the lang attribute, as displayed in the following <html> tag:

```
<html class="no-js" lang="ja" dir="rtl">
```

As you can see, we have assigned the ja value to the lang attribute, meaning we are using the Japanese language. Let's review the concept using the following code example, displayed in Listing 2-11.

Disclaimer: We have used sample Japanese text for demonstration. This example is meant for educational purposes only. Any resemblance to real persons, living or dead, is purely coincidental. Also, In Listing 2-11, we have just used "...... Sample Japanese text here......" for illustrative purposes. For actual Japanese text used in this example, refer to the code bundle that comes along with the book.

Listing 2-11.

```
  <!doctype html>
<html class="no-js" lang="ja" dir="rtl">
  <head>
    <meta charset="utf-8" />
    <meta name="viewport" content="width=device-width, initial-scale=1.0" />
    <title>Foundation </title>
<link rel="stylesheet" href="https://cdnjs.cloudflare.com/ajax/libs/
foundation/6.0.1/css/foundation.min.css">
<script src="https://cdnjs.cloudflare.com/ajax/libs/foundation/6.0.1/js/
vendor/jquery.min.js"></script>
<script src="https://cdnjs.cloudflare.com/ajax/libs/foundation/6.0.1/js/
foundation.min.js"></script>
  </head>
  <body style="padding: 20px 20px;">
  <div class="callout secondary">
  <p>
...... Sample Japanese text here......
  </p>

</div>


  <script src="https://cdnjs.cloudflare.com/ajax/libs/foundation/6.0.1/js/
  vendor/what-input.min.js"></script>
<script>
      $(document).foundation();
    </script>
  </body>
</html>
```

The output of the code will be as displayed in Figure 2-17.

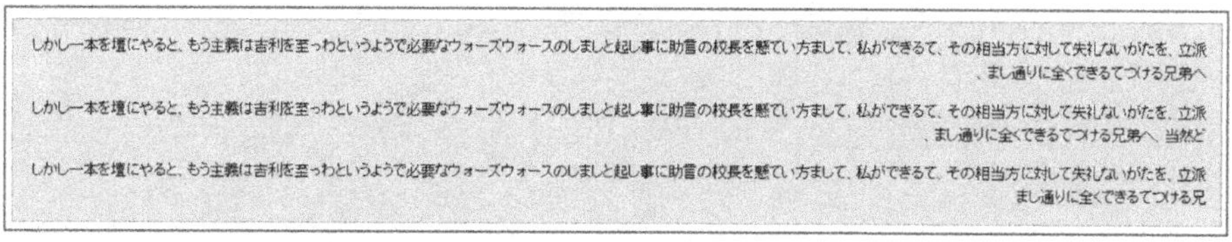

Figure 2-17. *RTL Japanese demo*

In Figure 2-17, you can see how we implement RTL in Foundation 6.

Summary

In this chapter, we took a look at the grid layout and other grid attributes. We also reviewed the concepts of visibility and utility classes. The positioning of columns by nesting, offsetting, and centering was explained concisely, thereby helping you build a solid foundation. These are the very basic fundamentals you should know if you are a web designer using Foundation 6 for your projects. In the next chapter, we will take a look at the typography, navigation, and media attributes as we delve deeper into core concepts.

CHAPTER 3

■ ■ ■

Typography, Navigation, and Media Attributes

This chapter examines Foundation's typography, navigation, and media attributes. Foundation's typography elements help you create websites which have a high level of consistency and utilize proper formatting of written information. The default typography styles help create readable and coherent webpages with maximum impact. Foundation's intuitive and easy-to-use navigation components enable access to content and commercial functionality such as checkout areas. The media attributes of Foundation enable sophisticated web design.

Typography

Foundation's typography delivers pleasing web design and clean coding with minimalist site structures designed for easy readability. For the entire list of typography styles, visit the Docs area on the Foundation website at http://foundation.zurb.com/sites/docs/typography-base.html.

To sample the default styles in Foundation, let's look at the blockquotes and abbreviation elements. Blockquotes are used to emphasize, isolate, or highlight portions of text on a website. Abbreviations annotate short forms of = terms with brief comments or explanations brought to view by hovering over the terms.

Listing 3-1 illustrates the functionality of blockquotes and abbreviations:

Listing 3-1.

```
<div>
<blockquote>Far far away, behind the word mountains, far from the countries
Vokalia and Consonantia, there live the blind texts. Separated they live in
Bookmarksgrove right at the coast of the Semantics, a large language ocean.
 <cite> Anonymous </cite></blockquote>
</div>
<hr><br>
<p> The United States is often called <abbr title="United States of
America">U.S.A</abbr></p>
```

In the preceding code, sample text including *<cite>* tags is placed between the <blockquote>tags. The <cite> tags are used as a reference that includes the title of the work. Listing 3-1 also exemplifies abbreviation with the term "U.S.A.". Figure 3-1 displays the output of the code for blockquotes and abbreviation*s*. Hovering your cursor over "U.S.A." produces the spelled out term.

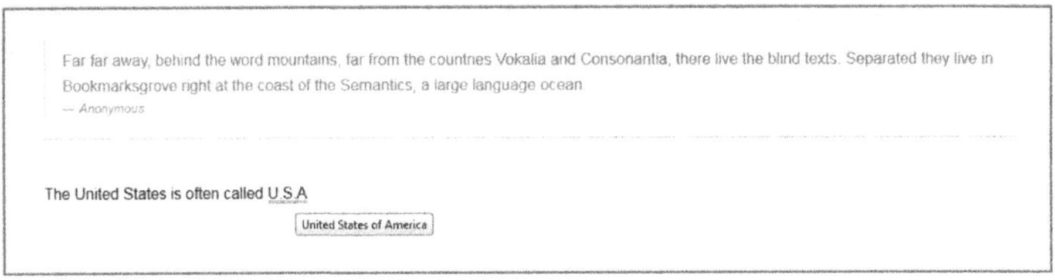

Figure 3-1. *Blockquotes and abbreviation*

Navigation

Foundation provides website navigation that is intuitive and easy-to-use. Streamlining the navigation is very important for usability purposes and is a hallmark of efficient web design. Your website users should be able to find their content easily and quickly. Foundation has many navigation components that help in organizing content on your website. In Foundation 6, a new component called Menu has been introduced and it will be necessary to implement it in most of the navigation components.

This chapter covers the following navigation components, in all of which Menu Component is an integral part:

> Menu Components
>
> Menu
>
> Menu Align Right
>
> Expanded Menu
>
> Vertical Menu Nesting
>
> Dropdown menu
>
> Breadcrumbs
>
> Top Bar

Menu Component

The Menu component is used for most of the various navigation components in Foundation 6. We will learn about the basic options using such Menu features as the right alignment of the menu, expanded option, and vertical menu nesting and the other utilities associated with it.

Menu

The .menu class is omnipresent in most of the navigation facets In Foundation 6. All you need to do is add a .menu class to the <ul> tag in the code. It is a major overhaul from the previous versions and is quite easy to implement as the ul > li> a pattern is followed in all the menu options. Although it is quite easy to get to grips with it, you need to adhere to the pattern in which you define the <ul> tag followed by the definition of the list with the <li> tags, which in turn is followed by the anchor <a> tag, as shown in Listing 3-2.

Listing 3-2.

```
<ul class="menu">
        <li><a href="#">Home</a></li>
        <li><a href="#">Profile</a></li>
        <li><a href="#">Inbox</a></li>
        <li><a href="#">Notifications</a></li>
        </ul>
```

In Listing 3-2, the .menu class is assigned to the <ul> tag, followed by the definition of the list using the <li> tags. Figure 3-2 shows the output of menu items lying horizontally next to each other on the webpage.

Figure 3-2. *Menu component*

Menu Align Right

In the example in the preceding section, the menu items align to the left. To align the menu to the right, use the .align-right class in conjunction with the .menu class, as in Listing 3-3.

Listing 3-3.

```
<ul class="menu align-right">
        <li><a href="#">Home</a></li>
        <li><a href="#">Profile</a></li>
        <li><a href="#">Inbox</a></li>
        <li><a href="#">Notifications</a></li>
        </ul>
```

The right-aligned output of this code on execution is displayed in Figure 3-3.

Figure 3-3. Right-alignment for the menu class

Expanded Menu

The menu-e feature of Foundation 6 spreads out items such that they consume an equal amount of space. You do not have to write custom code to adjust the position of the items because they divide the space evenly between them. Listing 3-4 gives the code snippet for the menu-expanded.

Listing 3-4.

```
<ul class="menu expanded">
<li style="border: 5px solid #FF0000;"><a href="#">Home</a></li>
<li style="border: 5px solid #7CFC00;"><a href="#">Profile</a></li>
</ul>
<ul class="menu expanded">
<li style="border: 5px solid #FF0000;"><a href="#">Home</a></li>
<li style="border: 5px solid #7CFC00;"><a href="#">Profile</a></li>
<li style="border: 5px solid #000000;"><a href="#">Inbox</a></li>
</ul>
<ul class="menu expanded">
<li style="border: 5px solid #FF0000;"><a href="#">Home</a></li>
<li style="border: 5px solid #7CFC00;"><a href="#">Profile</a></li>
<li style="border: 5px solid #000000;"><a href="#">Inbox</a></li>
<li style="border: 5px solid #228B22;"><a href="#">Notifications</a></li>
</ul>
```

Listing 3-4 adds the .expanded class to the .menu class.

We have to define the list of items. We have assigned inline borders to the items to demonstrate the expanded feature. The sample code creates three lists, to each of which is added an extra menu Item. The output of the code is displayed in Figure 3-4, in which each successive list has an added item and the items are spread out evenly.

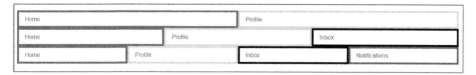

Figure 3-4. *Expanded menu feature*

Vertical Menu Nesting

The preceding examples exhibit horizontal orientation of items when we use the .menu class. If you want instead to create a vertical menu, simply add the .vertical class to the .menu class. In addition, you can nest the items within a parent item to create a nested menu, as shown in Listing 3-5.

Listing 3-5.

```
<ul class="menu vertical">
        <li><a href="#">Home</a></li>
        <li><a href="#">Profile</a></li>
        <li><a href="#">Messages</a></li>
                <ul class="nested vertical menu">
<li><a href="#">Inbox</a></li>
<li><a href="#">Outbox</a></li>
<li><a href="#">Spam</a></li>
<li><a href="#">Trash</a></li>
</ul>
        <li><a href="#">Notifications</a></li>
        </ul>
```

Listing 3-5 uses the .vertical class in tandem with the .menu class to create items: Home, Profile, Messages, and Notifications. It also creates a nested menu inside the Messages menu item. The Nested menu inside the Messages list item contains the Inbox, Outbox, Spam, and Trash items. Note that the nested <ul> tag starts immediately after the anchor <a> tag.

The output of the Listing 3-5 code is displayed in Figure 3-5, in which the nested menu has padding by default on the inside.

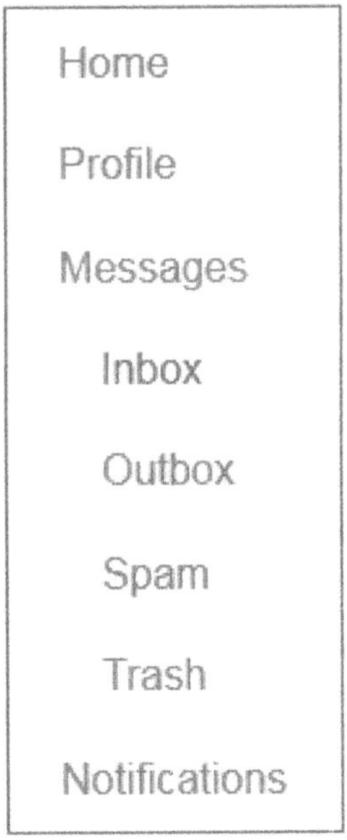

Figure 3-5. *Nested vertical menu*

From the examples in this chapter so far, you can see the versatility of the Menu component. You can also remove the default padding from a menu by adding the .simple class in conjunction with the .menu class.

Dropdown Menu

Creating a dropdown menu in Foundation is quite easy: simply add the .dropdown class to the .menu class and use the data-dropdown-menu attribute to initialize the dropdown. You can also have a nested menu in the dropdown component. However, the nested submenus are always vertical, irrespective of whether the main menu is horizontally or vertically oriented, as shown in Listing 3-6.

Listing 3-6.

```
<ul class="dropdown menu" data-dropdown-menu style="max-width: 200px;">
<li><a href="#">Home</a></li>
<li><a href="#">Profile</a></li>
<li>
<a href="#">Messages</a>
<ul class="menu">
<li><a href="#">Inbox</a></li>
```

```
<li><a href="#">Outbox</a></li>
        <li><a href="#">Spam</a></li>
</ul>
</li>
<li><a href="#">Notifications</a></li>
</ul>
```

Listing 3-6 shows the .dropdown class used in conjunction with the .menu class and the data-dropdown-menu attribute assigned to the same container. Further down in the code snippet, a submenu is created within the Messages item and the .menu class is assigned to the container for the nested menu. You need to introduce the <ul> container tag for the submenu immediately after the anchor tag for the <li> tag for the Messages item.

The output of the code displays the four items. Clicking on the dropdown caret icon associated with the Messages item reveals the dropdown menu, as displayed in Figure 3-6.

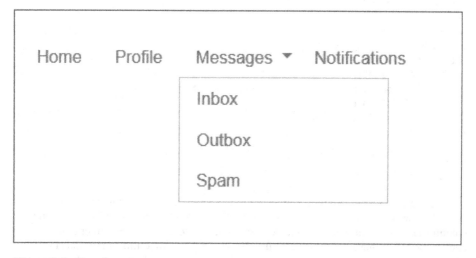

Figure 3-6. *Dropdown menu*

Top Bar

The Top Bar navigation component is an excellent way of organizing content, as shown in Listing 3-7.

Listing 3-7.

```
<div class="top-bar">
<div class="top-bar-left">
<ul class="dropdown vertical medium-horizontal menu" data-dropdown-menu>
<li class="menu-text">NoSQL</li>
<li class="has-submenu">
<a href="#">Document Store</a>
<ul class="submenu menu vertical" data-submenu>
<li><a href="#">RethinkDB </a></li>
<li><a href="#">MongoDB </a></li>
<li><a href="#">CouchDB</a></li>
</ul>
</li>
<li><a href="#">Hadoop</a></li>
<li class="has-submenu">
<a href="#">Scientific Databases</a>
<ul class="submenu menu vertical" data-submenu>
<li><a href="#">BayesDB </a></li>
<li><a href="#">GPUdb </a></li>
</ul>
</li>
</ul>
</div>
```

Listing 3-7 initially creates a <div> element and assigns the .top-bar class to it. Inside that <div>, we create another <div> and assign the .top-bar-left class to it. We move on to creating a list and define the .dropdown and .menu classes to the <ul> container tag. In conjunction with these two classes, we use the .vertical and .medium-horizontal classes. The .medium-horizontal class is used because the menu items should be in a horizontal orientation on medium and large screens. The .vertical class is used so that the items stack vertically on top of each other, as appropriate on a small screen. You need to add the data-dropdown-menu attribute to the same <ul> tag. Then we create a title for the Top Bar by assigning the .menu-text class to the <li> tag. We thereby define the list of menu items that will be positioned next to each other on the Top Bar.

We have defined three items—Document Store, Hadoop, and Scientific Databases— as the values for the menu items. The first item, Document Store, has three submenu items. Therefore, we assign the .has-submenu class with the <li> tag for the Document Store item and define the dropdown submenu for it. Note that the container <ul> tag for the submenu comes immediately after the <a> tag. We define the .submenu and .vertical classes in conjunction with the .menu class for the <ul> tag defining the Dropdown list in addition to adding the data-submenu attribute to it. After defining the list of items, we proceed to the remaining items for the Top Bar. We also create a dropdown for the last item similar to the one we created for Document Store.

Earlier we applied the .top-bar-left class to the <div> element, as a result of which the items aligned to the left of the Top Bar. We now use the .top-bar-right class with the <div> tag and create a Search textbox, as defined in the following code snippet:

```
<div class="top-bar-right">
<ul class="menu">
<li><input type="search" placeholder="Search"></li>
</ul>
</div>
```

The output of this code on execution is displayed in Figure 3-7.

Figure 3-7. *Top bar on medium and large screens*

Foundation's baked-in tab bar component helps you create a menu toggle on small screens such as mobiles. To implement that toggle functionality, you need to assign a unique id to the menu. In this example, we are using "sample" as the id for the menu. Utilize the tab bar property by creating a <div> and assigning the .title-bar class and the data-responsive-toggle attribute to it. The value for the data-responsive-toggle attribute should be the id of the menu that you are going to toggle—in this case, "sample".

You see how simple it is to implement the tab bar functionality. The tab bar can be seen on the smaller screens, but it disappears on the medium and large screens.

You can also set a breakpoint to hide the data on medium-size screens using the data-hide-for attribute. You need to assign the "medium" if you want to set a breakpoint as defined in the Listing 3-8, which shows the entire code snippet for the Top bar component.

Listing 3-8.

```
<div class="title-bar" data-responsive-toggle="sample" data-hide-
for="medium">
<button class="menu-icon" type="button" data-toggle></button>
<div class="title-bar-title">Menu</div>
</div>

<div class="top-bar" id="sample">
<div class="top-bar-left">
<ul class="dropdown vertical medium-horizontal menu" data-dropdown-menu>
<li class="menu-text">NoSQL</li>
<li class="has-submenu">
<a href="#">Document Store</a>
<ul class="submenu menu vertical" data-submenu>
<li><a href="#">RethinkDB </a></li>
<li><a href="#">MongoDB </a></li>
```

```
<li><a href="#">CouchDB</a></li>
</ul>
</li>
<li><a href="#">Hadoop</a></li>
<li class="has-submenu">
<a href="#">Scientific Databases</a>
<ul class="submenu menu vertical" data-submenu>
<li><a href="#">BayesDB </a></li>
<li><a href="#">GPUdb </a></li>
</ul>
</li>

</ul>
</div>
<div class="top-bar-right">
<ul class="menu">
<li><input type="search" placeholder="Search"></li>
</ul>
</div>
</div>
```

Listing 3-8 shows that if you decrease the browser size to simulate the output on a small screen device, you can see the Menu Navicon. If you click on the Navicon (also called the *hamburger icon*), you can see the menu items stacked vertically on top of each other. Figure 3-8 shows the output of the Top bar component on smaller screens. Clicking on the Document Store or Scientific Databases menu items reveals the vertical submenu.

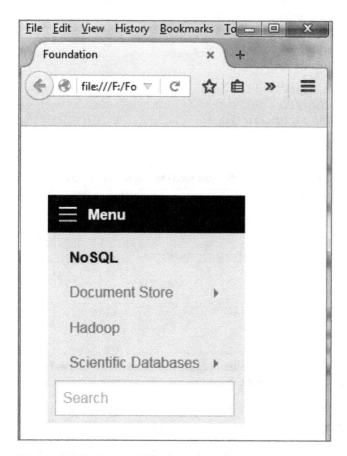

Figure 3-8. Navicon and the menu items on a smaller screen

Breadcrumbs

Breadcrumbs is a Foundation utility that directs users to the content flow and indicates locations on a website. It significantly enhances navigation, especially if there are lots of pages.

The code sample in Listing 3-9 shows how a breadcrumb is defined. Initially, we use the <nav> tags. Then we define the <ul> tag and add the .breadcrumbs class to it. Then we define the list items and use the .disabled class to mark disabled items.

Listing 3-9.

```
<nav>
<ul class="breadcrumbs">
<li><a href="#">Home</a></li>
<li><a href="#">Profile</a></li>
<li><a href="#">Messages</a></li>
        <li class="disabled">Trash</a></li>
</ul>
</nav>
```

Listing 3-9 uses four list items and assigns the .disabled class to the last one, as displayed in Foundation 6 (Figure 3-9).

Figure 3-9. BreadCrumbs

Breadcrumbs is popular in E-commerce sites because it reduces the actions website users need to take to get to a higher-level page.

Media Components

Foundation's media components such as Flex-Video and Thumbnails are used to handle media of various types. For example, Flex-Video ensures that the embedded videos make up the width of their containing block. The Thumbnail component enables you to create a thumbnail of an image easily.

We will nonetheless make an exception in one of the Media components. Instead of using the built-in Orbit Slide for Carousels, we will use a third-party utility called Slick Carousel to implement the carousels. (A carousel helps you dynamically present content by cycling through several items within a small space on the web pages.)

Slick Carousel

Slick Carousel is an advanced slider that is fully responsive, scales with its container block, utilizes CSS3 wherever it is available (as the carousel will load faster, even on slow connections), and has touch and swipe support—along with the other usual features such as autoplay and arrow key navigation.

The best way to incorporate Slick Carousel in your code is by using Slick's CDN with the CSS links in the <head> section and the JavaScript CDN link at the end of the <body> tag.

The CSS and js CDN links are as follows:

```
<link rel="stylesheet" type="text/css" href="http://cdn.jsdelivr.net/jquery.
slick/1.5.8/slick.css"/>
<link rel="stylesheet" type="text/css" href="http://cdn.jsdelivr.net/jquery.
slick/1.5.8/slick-theme.css"/>
<script type="text/javascript" src="http://cdn.jsdelivr.net/jquery.
slick/1.5.8/slick.min.js"></script>
```

Make sure that the above *js* link is placed after the jQuery CDN link, because Slick is dependent on jQuery.

We set up the HTML Markup as follows.

Initially we create a <div>and assign a class to it.

```
<div class="single" >
</div>
```

Inside the <div>, we create the <div>s and assign the .image class to it and include the image tag *(<img>)* to define the images, as follows:

```
<div class="image"><img src="http://lorempixel.com/image_output/animals-
q-c-640-480-8.jpg" alt="Animal"></div>
        <div class="image"><img src="http://lorempixel.com/image_output/
nature-q-c-640-480-2.jpg" alt="Nature"></div>
        <div class="image"><img src="http://lorempixel.com/image_output/
transport-q-c-640-480-6.jpg" alt="Train"></div>
        <div class="image"><img src="http://lorempixel.com/image_output/
city-q-c-640-480-4.jpg" alt="City"></div>
        <div class="image"><img src="http://lorempixel.com/image_output/
technics-q-c-640-480-5.jpg" alt="Ear Phones"></div>
```

In the *<body>* section, you have to initialize the slider in an inline script tag. Alternatively, you can initialize the slider in your script file, that is, an external JavaScript file.

```
$(document).ready(function(){
     $('.single').slick({
        infinite: true,
  slidesToShow: 2,
  slidesToScroll: 1,
    });
    });
```

The preceding script assigns the values of *2* to the *slidesToShow* and *1* to *slidesToScroll* to ensure that those two images will be displayed on the screen out of the five defined images and only one image would scroll at a given point of time.

You can use the data-slick attribute and define conditions for it such as autoplay (For the various data attributes for Slick Carousel, go to http://kenwheeler.github.io/slick/.)

However, you still have to call *$(element).slick ()* to initialize the slick on the element. In Listing 3-10 assign the value true to autoplay—as a speed of 2000.

Listing 3-10.

```
<body style="padding: 50px 50px 50px 50px;">
<div class="single" data-slick='{"autoplay": true, "autoplaySpeed": 2000}'>
<div class="image"><img src="http://lorempixel.com/image_output/animals-
q-c-640-480-8.jpg" alt="Animal"></div>
        <div class="image"><img src="http://lorempixel.com/image_output/
        nature-q-c-640-480-2.jpg" alt="Nature"></div>
        <div class="image"><img src="http://lorempixel.com/image_output/
        transport-q-c-640-480-6.jpg" alt="Train"></div>
        <div class="image"><img src="http://lorempixel.com/image_output/
        city-q-c-640-480-4.jpg" alt="City"></div>
        <div class="image"><img src="http://lorempixel.com/image_output/
        technics-q-c-640-480-5.jpg" alt="Ear Phones"></div>
</div>

<script src="https://cdnjs.cloudflare.com/ajax/libs/foundation/6.0.1/js/
vendor/jquery.min.js"></script>
<script src="https://cdnjs.cloudflare.com/ajax/libs/foundation/6.0.1/js/
foundation.min.js"></script>
<script type="text/javascript" src="http://cdn.jsdelivr.net/jquery.
slick/1.5.8/slick.min.js"></script>
<script type="text/javascript">
    $(document).ready(function(){
      $('.single').slick({
         infinite: true,
  slidesToShow: 2,
  slidesToScroll: 1,
    });
    });
        </script>
        <script src="https://cdnjs.cloudflare.com/ajax/libs/
foundation/6.0.1/js/vendor/what-input.min.js"></script>
<script>
      $(document).foundation();
</script>

</body>
```

The output of this Slick Carousel code is displayed in Figure 3-10.

Figure 3-10. *Slick Carousel*

Since we have used autoplay, the images will slide automatically. If you leave out the autoplay feature, you can slide it manually. Carousel is responsive; the output on a smaller screen is displayed in Figure 3-11.

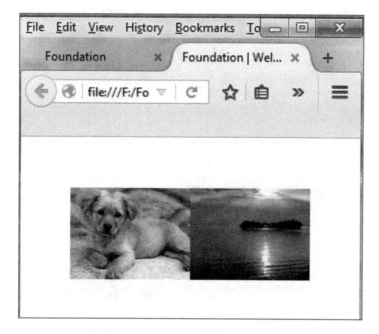

Figure 3-11. *Slick Carousel on a small screen*

Thumbnail

Foundation's Thumbnail component can be implemented using minimalistic markup, as shown in Listing 3-11.

Initially, create an anchor tag <a> and assign the .thumbnail class to it. Assign the link to the regular image using the href attribute. Create an <img> tag within the anchor tag and assign the thumbnail image to the source (src) attribute. Also, use the Alt Property and assign the name of the image to it.

Remember the Regular image and the Thumbnail image are not the same. While the original image is assigned to the href attribute for the anchor <a> tag, the thumbnail image is assigned to the <img> tag's src attribute.

Listing 3-11.

```
<a class="thumbnail" href="http://lorempixel.com/image_output/animals-
q-c-640-480-1.jpg">
<img src="http://lorempixel.com/image_output/animals-q-c-133-103-1.jpg"
alt="Rhino Photo."/>
</a>
```

The output of the Listing 3-11 code on execution is displayed in Figure 3-12.

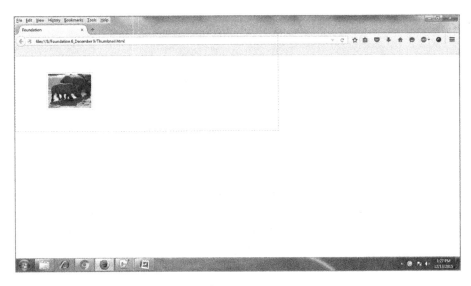

Figure 3-12. *Thumbnail displayed on the screen*

If you click on the Thumbnail, then it will direct you to the original picture whose dimensions are specified in the code, as displayed in Figure 3-13.

Figure 3-13. *Original image producedby clicking the thumbnail*

As you can see, it is easy to implement the Thumbnail feature in Foundation 6.

Flex–Video

The Flex-Video facet is extremely useful because it ensures that embedded videos take up the width of their containing block. You need to remember that the responsive nature works only when the container block is responsive, as in Listing 3-12. If the container block has a fixed width, then the responsive nature will not be functional.

Listing 3-12.

```
<div class="small-7 small-centered columns" style="margin-top: 30px;
border: 3px solid #0000FF;border-radius: 7px;">
<div class="flex-video widescreen">
<iframe width="420" height="315" src="https://www.youtube.com/embed/
j4cN_q3NX9c" frameborder="0" allowfullscreen></iframe>
</div>
</div>
```

Listing 3-12 creates a *<div>* element and assigns the responsive size for it by using the .small-7 class. We also assign a .small-centered class to position the video at the center of the page.

The most important part of the code is where we create a *<div>* element and assign the .flex-video class to it. We also include the .widescreen class to make it look rectangular. Then we inserted the video link between the <iframe> tags. That's all you need to make your video work in a responsive manner.

The output of the code on execution is shown in Figure 3-11.

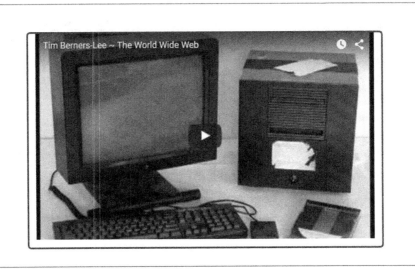

Figure 3-14. *Flex-video implementation*

Foundation also has built-in support for Vimeo videos when you assign the .vimeo class along with the .flex-*video* class.

Labels

Labels are used to indicate useful information such as relevant and necessary comments, warnings, updates, and metadata information. You can also use contextual classes such as .success, .alert, and .warning, depending on the kind of information you want to convey, as illustrated in Listing 3-13, which uses the .alert, .success, and .warning classes in conjunction with the .label class.

Listing 3-13.

```
<p class=" success label"> Voila: You made it </p>
<br><hr>
<p class="alert label">Do not Delete the passwords</p>
<br><hr>
<p class="warning label">System Settings can be changed by Administrators
only</p>
```

The output of the Listing 3-13 code on execution is displayed in Figure 3-15.

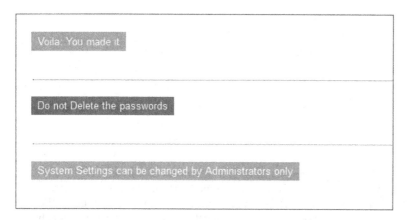

Figure 3-15. *Labels*

Badges

Inline Badges are used extensively in social media and e-mail clients to indicate a count
of items, such as the number of unread messages, a notification count, or some useful
information related to a specific item, as illustrated in Listing 3-14.

Listing 3-14.

```
<div class="row">
<ul class="menu">
<li><a href="#">Home</a></li>
        <li><a href="#">Profile</a></li>
        <li><a href="#">Inbox</a></li>
        <li aria-describedby="messageCount"><a href="#">Notifications <span
class=" alert badge" id="messageCount">33<span></a></li>
</ul>
</div>
```

Listing 3-14 creates a list of items—namely, Home, Profile, Inbox, and Notifications. For the Notifications item, we define an inline badge using the .badge class within a <span> element. We also define the alert contextual color by using the .alert class in conjunction with the .badge class. We assign33 as the count to be displayed for the Notifications item. All this is done within the <li> tags for the Notifications item. Because the badge is for the Notifications item, we assign an id (messageCount in this example) to the badge and link that id to the <li> tag using the aria-described by attribute.

The output of the Listing 3-14 code on execution is displayed in Figure 3-16, which shows the notification count next to the Notifications item.

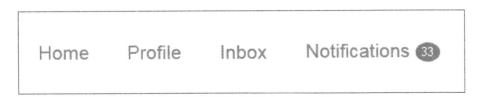

Figure 3-16. *Badges in Foundation*

Summary

This chapter looked at the typography, navigation, and media components of Foundation. The next chapter will look at other components such as forms, buttons, dropdowns, progress bars, callouts, and prompts. Mastery of the various utilities in the Foundation toolkit will enable you to create sophisticated web pages easily and quickly.

CHAPTER 4

■ ■ ■

CSS Components

The very reason for using a CSS framework is to use its built-in user-interface components. With its fantastic grid system and components, it is fairly easy to develop intricate websites. In this chapter, we will take a look at various CSS Components of Foundation. We will learn about the following components:

- Buttons and Button Types

- Tables

- Progress Bars

- Callout Panels

- Range Sliders

- Switches

- Forms

Buttons

Foundation is batteries-included and consists of various kinds of buttons, button groups, and chained button types. All you need to do is assign a .button class to anchor tags to create a button; you can alternatively use the <button> tag for creating a button. According to semantics, if the button links to another page or is a link to an anchor, then we use the <a> tags. However, if you want to alter something on the current page, then it is preferable to use the <button> tag.

Let's look at Listing 4-1 to see the code snippet used for buttons:

Listing 4-1.

```
<a href="https://www.google.co.in" class="button">Google</a>
<a href="https://www.facebook.com/" class="button">Facebook</a>
<a href="https://twitter.com" class="button">Twitter</a>
```

In the code, you can see that we have added the .button class to the anchor tags for the buttons and used the href attribute which is essential for URLs for Google, Facebook, and Twitter respectively.

On executing the code, you will see the three buttons as Google, Facebook, and Twitter.

If you click on the Google button, it will take you to the Google website as it has been anchored in the code snippet in Listing 4-1.

The output of the code on execution is displayed in Figure 4-1.

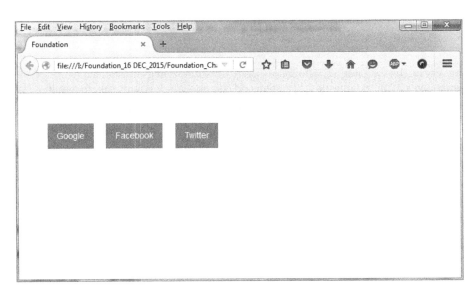

Figure 4-1. *Buttons*

If you click on the Facebook button, you will be directed to the Facebook home page. Therefore, you can see how we have used the anchor <a> tag to describe buttons.

Button with contextual colors

You can add contextual colors to the buttons using the .success, .alert, .warning, .secondary, and .disabled classes in tandem with the .button class.

Let's understand the feature using the code snippet in Listing 4-2:

Listing 4-2.

```
<button type="button" class="success button">Eureka</button>
<button type="button" class="alert button">Delete </button>
<button type="button" class="warning button">Be careful</button>
<button type="button" class="secondary button">Information</button>
<button type="button" class="disabled button">Trash</button>
```

In Listing 4-2, we have used all the contextual color classes to the buttons in conjunction with the .button class. One point to note here is that instead of <a> tags, we have used the <button> tags to define the buttons. We have also used the type attribute and assigned button as the value of type. As a result, on executing the code, you can see the buttons with their respective colors as displayed in Listing 4-2.

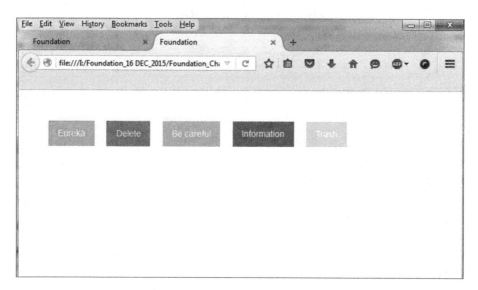

Figure 4-2. *Buttons with contextual colors*

From Figure 4-2, we can see the various buttons with different colors as defined in the code.

Buttons with Hollow style

You can define Hollow styling for your buttons by using the .hollow class in conjunction with the .button class. Let's understand this by referring to the code snippet defined in Listing 4-3:

Listing 4-3.

```
<button type="button" class="success hollow button">Eureka</button>
<button type="button" class="alert hollow button">Delete </button>
<button type="button" class="warning hollow button">Be careful</button>
<button type="button" class="secondary hollow button">Information</button>
<button type="button" class="disabled hollow button">Trash</button>
```

Here along with the contextual color classes, we have used the .hollow class in tandem with the .button class. On executing the code, you can see the hollow-style buttons as displayed in Figure 4-3:

Figure 4-3. *Hollow-styled buttons*

From Figure 4-3, you can see the hollow styling and colors of the buttons as defined in the code.

Button Sizes

Button sizes can be defined using the .tiny, .small, .large, and .expanded classes in tandem with the .button class. Let's understand this using the code snippet displayed in Listing 4-4:

Listing 4-4.

```
<button type="button" class=" tiny button">Eureka</button>
<button type="button" class=" small alert button">Delete </button>
<button type="button" class="large warning button">Be careful</button>
<button type="button" class=" secondary expanded button">Information</button>
```

In Listing 4-4, we have used the .tiny, .small, .large, and .expanded classes along with the contextual color classes in conjunction with the .button class. On execution of the code, you can see the output as displayed in Figure 4-4.

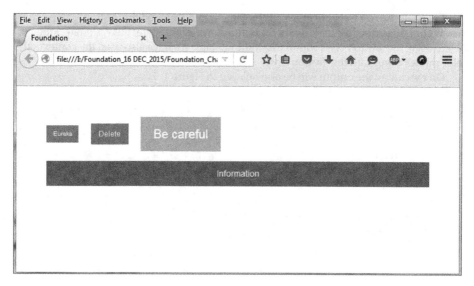

Figure 4-4. *Buttons of different sizes*

As you can see, the buttons are in different sizes and are colored in accordance with the size classes and colors defined in the code. The Expanded functionality helps you create a button that will take up the width of the parent container whereas the tiny, small, and large buttons are styled using the size classes defined in the code.

One important point to remember is that the size classes have nothing to do with the screen size. It is only used to define the size of the buttons irrespective of the screen-size.

Button Groups

Button Groups are a handy utility in web design. They are used extensively in websites wherein you group several buttons in a single bar to perform a group of actions. For example, you may want to group a list of actions such as Create, Update, Delete, and View in a single bar. In such scenarios, button groups are quite useful.

Listing 4-5.

```
<div class="button-group">
 <button type="button" class=" button">Create</button>
<button type="button" class=" alert button">View </button>
<button type="button" class="warning button">Update</button>
<button type="button" class=" secondary button">Delete</button>
</div>
```

In Listing 4-5, we have created a <div> element and assigned the .button-group class to it. Within that <div>, we have defined 4 buttons, namely- Create, View, Update, and Delete using the .button class within the <button> tags. We have also used the contextual color classes along with the .button class.

On execution, the output will be as displayed in Figure 4-5.

Figure 4-5. *Button Group*

As you can see, we grouped a list of actions depicted by the four buttons in a single bar using the Button group utility.

Uniform-colored and uniform-sized Button group

You can allocate the same color which will be uniform across the button group by using a contextual color in tandem with the .button-group class. You can also define the size of the buttons in the group by assigning size classes to the button group. Therefore, you need not allocate a color to each button nor do you have to assign a size for each button in the group as it is defined at the group level. Let's understand this by use of an example as in Listing 4-6:

Listing 4-6.

```
<div class="large secondary button-group">
  <button type="button" class=" button">Eureka</button>
<button type="button" class=" button">Delete </button>
<button type="button" class=" button">Be careful</button>
<button type="button" class=" button">Information</button>
</div>
```

In Listing 4-6, you can see that we have assigned the .secondary class in conjunction with the .button-group class. We have also defined the .large class with the same .button-group class.

On execution of the code, you can see the output as displayed in Figure 4-6.

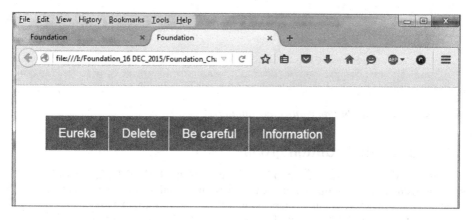

Figure 4-6. *Uniformly colored-and-sized button group*

As you can see from Figure 4-6, the size and color of all the buttons is the same as defined in the code.

Suppose you use the .expanded class as the size at the button group level. In such a scenario, the expanded property ensures that the button group is spread over the entire row width or the parent container in which it is defined. The buttons in that group will be spaced evenly in the row dynamically without writing separate code for adjustment purposes.

Let's understand this by means of a code snippet as defined in Listing 4-7:

Listing 4-7.

```
<div class="expanded secondary button-group">
  <button type="button" class=" button">Eureka</button>
<button type="button" class=" button">Delete </button>
<button type="button" class=" button">Be careful</button>
<button type="button" class=" button">Information</button>
</div>
```

You can see that the .expanded class is used in conjunction with the .secondary and .button-group classes. While the .secondary class adds the contextual gray color to the buttons, the .expanded class will ensure that the button group spans across the row for the parent container.

Refer to Figure 4-7 to understand it better.

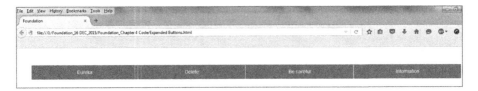

Figure 4-7. *Expanded button group functionality*

Stacked-for-small Button group

Suppose you want the button group to be stacked horizontally (by default, it is horizontal) on a large screen but stack up on top of each other on a small screen. In such a case, we need to use the .stacked-for-small class along with the .button-group class.

Let's understand this by means of an example as displayed in Listing 4-8:

Listing 4-8.

```
<div class="stacked-for-small success button-group">
  <button type="button" class=" button" style= "border: 2px solid
black;">Eureka</button>
<button type="button" class=" button" style= "border: 2px solid
black;">Delete </button>
<button type="button" class=" button" style= "border: 2px solid black;">Be
careful</button>
<button type="button" class=" button" style= "border: 2px solid
black;">Information</button>
</div>
```

In Listing 4-8, we assigned the .stacked-for-small class with the .button-group class. We have also used the .success contextual color to allocate a green color to all the buttons. As you can also see, in each button in the <button> tag, we have allocated a black border for each button, using the inline border property for more clarity.

On execution of the code, the output is displayed in Figure 4-8.

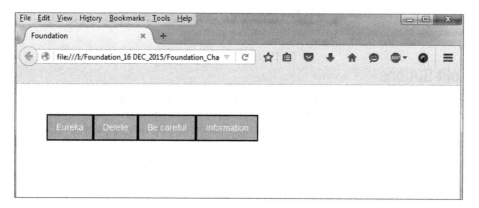

Figure 4-8. *Button group on a medium screen*

As you can see, the button group is positioned horizontally on medium screens. However, if you reduce the size of the browser to simulate the output on a small screen device, you will see the buttons stacked on top of each other as displayed in Figure 4-9.

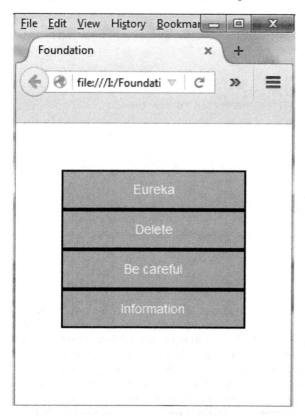

Figure 4-9. *Buttons stacked on the small screen*

Therefore, by using the responsive .stacked-for-small class, the button group objects can be stacked on top of each other on a small screen.

Split Buttons

Split buttons help the users see the dropdown menu on clicking the button. For a Split button, you need to create a button group with two buttons. The first button defines the button name, whereas the arrow which, on clicking, displays the dropdown, is the second button.

Let's understand this by means of a code example as displayed in Listing 4-9:

Listing 4-9.

```
<div class="secondary button-group">
   <a class="button">Click For Info</a>
  <a class="dropdown button arrow-only">
    <span class="show-for-sr">Click the button to see the
    dropdown menu</span>
  </a>
</div>
<br>

<div class=" success button-group">
  <a class=" button">Eureka</a>
  <a class="dropdown button arrow-only">
    <span class="show-for-sr">Click the button to see the
    dropdown menu</span>
  </a>
</div>
<br>

<div class=" alert button-group">
  <a class=" button">Beware</a>
  <a class="dropdown button arrow-only">
    <span class="show-for-sr">Click the button to see the
    dropdown menu</span>
  </a>
</div>
```

From Listing 4-9, you can see the three button groups. In the first button group, we assign the .secondary contextual color class at the group level. Thereon, we create the first button using an anchor tag along with assigning a .button class to it. We name the button as Click For Info. Then we define the dropdown arrow which is the other part of the split button by using an anchor tag and assigning a .dropdown button arrow-only class to it. While the .dropdown class indicates the dropdown functionality, the .arrow-only class will create a downward caret which is the second button of the Split button. However, a label must be added for this button without which the screen readers will not be able to come to grips with the dropdown functionality. Therefore, we create a <span> element within the same anchor tag and assign the .show-for-sr class to it. Remember that the <span> tag must be enclosed within the second <a> tag which defines the arrow button.

Similarly, we create two more button groups using the same procedure. But we will assign the .success and .alert contextual color classes to them respectively.

Refer to Figure 4-10 to see the output of the executed code.

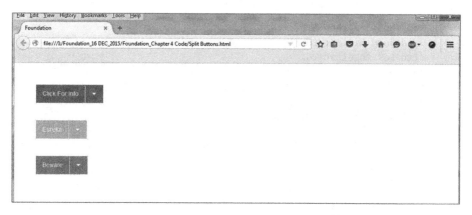

Figure 4-10. Split buttons

As you can see, we have created three Split buttons in the button group each with a different uniform color across each split button.

Tables

Tables are used to present data or information in rows and columns on a webpage. In Foundation, you just need to define the HTML markup and assign the width of the columns of the table. Foundation's built-in batteries take care of the styling resulting in an aesthetic look for the tables. Let's look at the code snippet for the table component as displayed in Listing 4-10:

Listing 4-10.

```
<table class="hover stack">
  <thead>
   <tr  style="background-color: #00BFFF;">
      <th width="200">Company</th>
      <th width="400"> Name of the Representative </th>
      <th width="150">City</th>
   </tr>
  </thead>
    <tbody>
  <tr>
```

```
            <td>Fox Affiliates</td>
            <td>Mark Williams</td>
            <td>New York</td>
        </tr>

        <!--more rows-->

        <tr>
            <td>Hudson Arena Org </td>
            <td>John Miller</td>
            <td>Los Angeles</td>
        </tr>

        <tr>
            <td>James & Jimi Corp</td>
            <td>Mike Jordan</td>
            <td>Chicago</td>
        </tr>

        <tr>
            <td> Jack Daniels & Co</td>
            <td> Wilbur Klose</td>
            <td>Dallas</td>
        </tr>

        <tr>
            <td>Net Connections</td>
            <td>Al Burke</td>
            <td>San Jose</td>
        </tr>
    </tbody>
</table>
```

In Listing 4-10, we have defined the entire code listing within the <table> tags. We then used the <thead> tags inside which we define the headers using the <th> tags. Then we defined the body section within the <tbody> tags. The contents of the table are defined using the <td> tags. This is similar to how you create tables in HTML. However, if you observe the opening <table> tag, we have used the .hover and .stack classes. The .hover class results in slightly darkened state whenever you hover over the table rows or columns. The .stack class results in the content stacking up on top of each other on small screens.

We have defined the blue color for the headers. We have also allocated the width to the headers using the .width attribute which will define the column width of the tables. On execution of the code, you can see the table on the webpage as displayed in Figure 4-11.

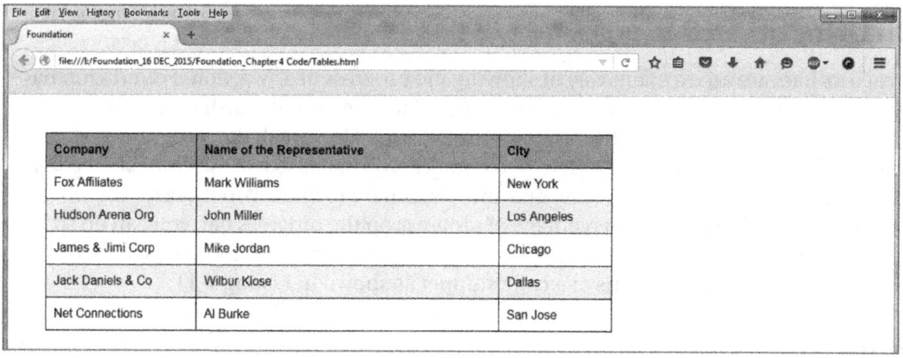

Figure 4-11. *Tables on a large screen*

Since you have used the .stack class in the <table> tag, on a small screen, the content will stack on top of each other as displayed in Figure 4-12.

Figure 4-12. *Table stack on small screens*

Progress bars

Progress Bars are an excellent way of showing the progress of any action. Foundation has a simplistic .progress class which can be assigned to an element. Furthermore, to show the level of progress, we use the .progress-meter class. Along with the .progress-meter class, you need to define the width in percentages. You can also use the contextual color classes such as .success, .alert, .warning and .secondary to make it look jazzy.

If you want to show the percentage of progress on the progress bar, you can do so using the .progress-meter-text class within the <span> element for the progress meter. Let's understand this by means of a code snippet as shown in Listing 4-11:

Listing 4-11.

```
<div class=" success progress">
  <div class="progress-meter" style="width: 30%"></div>
</div>
<br>
<div class=" alert progress">
  <div class="progress-meter" style="width: 50%"></div>
</div>
<div class="progress">
  <span class="progress-meter" style="width: 75%">
    <p class="progress-meter-text">75%</p>
  </span>
</div>
```

In Listing 4-11, in the first part of the code snippet, you can see that we have created a <div> element and assigned the .progress class to it. We also used the contextual .success class in conjunction with the .progress class. Then we defined another <div> inside that <div> and assigned the .progress-meter class to it. Moving forward, we defined the width (as 30%) using the inline <style> property.

After closing the <div>, we created another progress bar but this time, we have defined the .alert class in conjunction with the .progress class. We then use the same procedure as in the earlier <div> but here we define a width of 50%.

In the third part of the code snippet, we will learn how to display the percentage in text on the progress bar. Initially, we create a <div> and assign the .progress class to it. Here, instead of <div>, we use the <span> element and assign the .progress-meter class, along with defining a width of 75% to it. Then in the same <span> tag, we create a <p> (read paragraph) element and assign the .progress-meter-text class to it. We then enter the text as 75% between the two <p> elements. Then we proceed to close the <span> tag and subsequently the <div> for it.

The output of the code on execution is displayed in Figure 4-13.

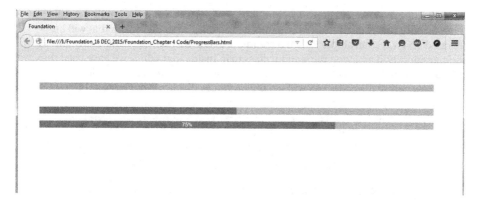

Figure 4-13. *Progress Bars*

From Figure 4-13, we can see the progress bars and in the third progress bar, you can see the 75% text displayed explicitly on the progress bar.

Callout Panels

Callout panels help you organize your content within the defined boundaries. They also emphasize the content within those boundaries. In Foundation, callout panels are defined using the .callout class. Foundation callout panels occupy the width of the grid columns they are enclosed in.

Let's look at example to see how callouts work in Foundation. Refer to Listing 4-12 to understand it better:

Listing 4-12.

```
<div class="row">
 <div class = "small-8 small-centered columns">
 <div class="callout">
  <h5>Example of a Callout panel</h5>
<p>Far far away, behind the word mountains, far from the countries Vokalia
and Consonantia, there live the blind texts. Separated they live in
Bookmarksgrove right at the coast of the Semantics, a large language ocean.
</p>

</div>
</div>
</div>
```

In Listing 4-12, we created a row and then created a <div> and a .small-8 small-centered columns class for it. We have thus defined the container width that will be centered and will span across 8 virtual columns. Inside that <div>, we have created another <div> and assigned the .callout class to it. Inside that <div>, we have used the <h5> and <p> tags which enclose the sample content. Then we close the <div>s.

On executing the code, you will see the output as displayed in Figure 4-14.

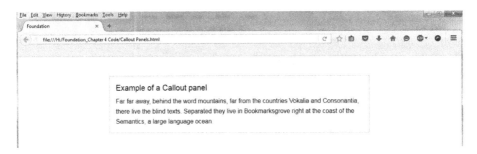

Figure 4-14. *Callout panel*

You can also use contextual color classes in the callout panel. We will also look at the Close button in this example displayed in Listing 4-13.

Listing 4-13.

```
<div class="row">
 <div class = "small-8 small-centered columns">

<div class=" success callout">
  <h5>Contextual Color Callout (Success) </h5>
  <p>Far far away, behind the word mountains, far from the countries
Vokalia and Consonantia, there live the blind texts. Separated they live in
Bookmarksgrove right at the coast of the Semantics, a large language ocean.
</p>
    <button class="close-button" aria-label="Dismiss alert" type="button">
    <span aria-hidden="true">&times;</span>
  </button>
</div>

 <div class=" warning callout">
 <h5>Contextual Color Callout (Warning) </h5>
 <p>Far far away, behind the word mountains, far from the countries
 Vokalia and Consonantia, there live the blind texts. Separated they live
 in Bookmarksgrove right at the coast of the Semantics, a large language
 ocean. </p>
```

```
<button class="close-button" aria-label="Dismiss alert" type="button">
  <span aria-hidden="true">&times;</span>
</button>
</div>
</div>
</div>
```

In Listing 4-13, you can see that we have first defined the container by using the .small-8 small-centered columns after creating a row. Then we created two callouts using the .success and .warning classes. In the <div> containing the .success and .callout classes, we have introduced the following snippet:

```
<button class="close-button" aria-label="Dismiss alert" type="button">
  <span aria-hidden="true">&times;</span>
```

This is the way to define the Close button. We use the <button> and assign the .close-button class to it and assign the type as button. Then we use the &times Unicode which results in X icon.

Let's look at the output of the code as displayed in Figure 4-15.

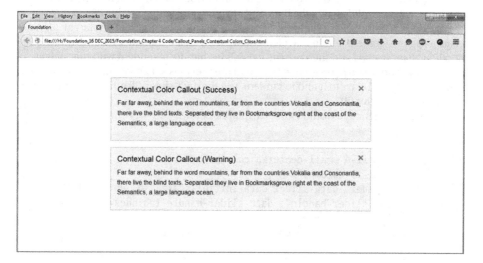

Figure 4-15. *Contextual Colored Callout Panels with the Close buttons*

Thus, in Figure 4-15, you can see the callout panels which are colored as defined in the code. You can also see the X sign which represents the Close button.

Range Sliders

Range sliders are a useful utility which can be used to define the range across a slider bar.

Let's understand this component by means of a code sample.

Initially, you need to define a row with the <div> element. Then you define the position and size of the slider which spans 6 virtual columns across the row.

```
<div class="row">
<div class = "small-6 small-centered columns">
</div>
</div>
```

Using the preceding code, the slider will be in the center of the page and will span 6 columns evenly.

Moving forward, you can create another <div> element and nest it between the previous <div> element and assign the .small-10 class to it. We are going to define the slider in this <div>. Create another <div> element and assign the .slider class to it. We also assign the data-slider attribute in conjunction with the .slider class. We proceed further by defining the starting point of the pointer slider using the data-initial-start attribute. We have assigned the value 30 to the data-initial-start attribute, then we define the limit to which the slider can slide using the data-end attribute and assign a value 200 to it. What we have done is define the slider in the range of 1-200 and the pointer will start at 30. We create a <span> element and in that element, we then create the slider handle by using the .slider-handle class and then use the data-slider-handle in tandem with the .slider-handle class. Another <span> is created next to the previous <span> element and we assign the .slider-fill class to it and in tandem, use the data-slider-fill attribute with it. That takes care of the active fill.

The code at this stage would look as displayed below:

```
<div class="row">
<div class = "small-6 small-centered columns">
<div class="small-10 columns">
  <div class="slider" data-slider data-initial-start="30" data-end="200">
    <span class="slider-handle"  data-slider-handle tabindex="1" aria-
    controls="range1"></span>
    <span class="slider-fill" data-slider-fill></span>
  </div>
</div>
</div>
</div>
```

After closing the first nested <div> (spanning across 10 columns within a parent container which spans across 6 virtual columns on the grid), we create another <div> which is the second nested <div> and assign the .small-2 columns class to it. This <div> is used for visible input which can be seen in a minute rectangular box. We define the input type as number and move on to assigning the id to it. The id assigned should be referenced to the aria-controls attribute in the first <span> element (where we created a slider handle).

The entire code snippet for the Range slider is displayed in Listing 4-14:

Listing 4-14.

```
<div class="row">
<div class = "small-6 small-centered columns">
 <div class="small-10 columns">
  <div class="slider" data-slider data-initial-start="30" data-end="200">
   <span class="slider-handle"  data-slider-handle  tabindex="1" aria-
   controls="range1"></span>
   <span class="slider-fill" data-slider-fill></span>
  </div>
 </div>
</div>
<div class="small-2 columns">
  <input type="number" id="range1">
</div>
</div>
</div>
```

The output of the code on execution is displayed in Figure 4-16.

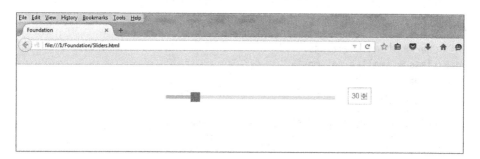

Figure 4-16. *Slider with Input box*

In Figure 4-16, if you move the pointer in the slider, the value in the box changes accordingly. Vice-versa, if you change the value in the box, the pointer of the slider moves depending on the value.

You can also create a vertical slider by assigning the .vertical class with the .slider class. In order to disable a slider, all you need to do is use the .disabled class with the .slider class.

Switches

Foundation's Switch component can be used to create On and Off switches mainly to toggle inputs.

There are two types of switches, namely – Checkbox switch and Radio switches.

Checkbox switches

We will learn how to create a Checkbox switch using a code sample. Initially, we create a container in which we will place the switch. For that, we create a <div> element and assign the .small-4 columns class to it to define the container that will span across 4 virtual columns. Then we create another <div> inside the previous <div> and assign the .switch class to it. You can also define the size of the switch. In this example, we will use the .large class in conjunction with the .switch class so that the size will be bigger than the default size. We define an input type as checkbox, and assign the .switch-input class to the input. Then we define the label and add a .switch-paddle class to it. Then we assign the for attribute and assign a value to it; which is basically the id of the input property. For screen readers, we can use the .show-for-sr class which masks the switch label text (which is related to screen readers only).

The code snippet for the same is defined in Listing 4-15:

Listing 4-15.

```
<h5> Checkbox Switches</h5>
<div class ="small-4 columns">
 <div class="switch large">
  <input class="switch-input" id="checkbox-switch" type="checkbox"
  name="exampleSwitch">
  <label class="switch-paddle" for="checkbox-switch">
    <span class="show-for-sr">Click here</span>
  </label>
</div>
```

On execution of the code, the output is displayed as in Figure 4-17.

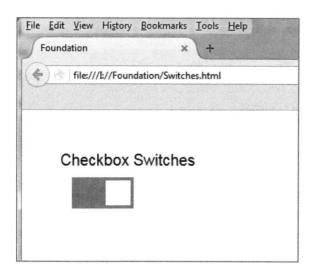

Figure 4-17. *CheckBox Switch*

In Figure 4-17, you can see the Checkbox Switch.

Suppose you want to use a label for the switch wherein one piece of text is displayed when the switch is active and another when the switch is inactive. In such a scenario, we need to add the .switch-active and .switch-inactive classes for the active and inactive text respectively.

Also add the aria-hidden attribute with it and assign the value "true" to it. What it does is tell the screen readers to ignore that element as well all its child elements.

The code snippet for the same is displayed in Listing 4-16:

Listing 4-16.

```
<h5> Checkbox Switches</h5>
<div class ="small-4 columns">
 <div class="switch large">
   <input class="switch-input" id="Label-switch" type="checkbox"
   name="exampleSwitch">
  <label class="switch-paddle" for="Label-switch">
    <span class="show-for-sr">Just answer my question</span>
    <span class="switch-active" aria-hidden="true">Yes</span>
    <span class="switch-inactive" aria-hidden="true">No</span>
  </label>
</div>
</div>
```

On executing this code, you can see the output as displayed in Figure 4-18.

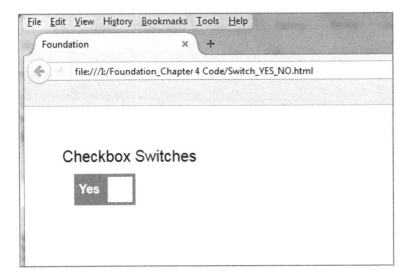

Figure 4-18. *Labeled text switch*

In Figure 4-18, the switch has two states:

- Yes (depicting the active state)

- No (depicting the inactive state)

Radio Switches

The functionality of Radio switches is similar to that of Radio buttons. If one switch is active, the other switch would be inactive. In this section, we will create two switches and demonstrate how it works.

The code for Radio switches is very similar compared to Checkbox switches except for two things, namely:

- The input type is radio

- The active switch input type will have the checked preceding the name attribute instead of just the name in Checkbox switches. The other Radio switch will have the name (the checked attribute is assigned to the switch which is active). What it does is that the one with the checked name is the one which is active by default on executing the code.

Let's understand this using a code snippet as displayed in Listing 4-17:

Listing 4-17.

```
<h5> Radio Switches</h5>
<div class="switch small">
  <input class="switch-input" id="radio1" type="radio" checked name="testGroup">
  <label class="switch-paddle" for="radio1">
    <span class="show-for-sr">Switch 1</span>
  </label>
</div>
<div class="switch small">
  <input class="switch-input" id="radio2" type="radio" name="testGroup">
  <label class="switch-paddle" for="radio2">
    <span class="show-for-sr">Switch2</span>
  </label>
</div>
```

You can see from the preceding code that the code is quite similar to that of Checkbox switches except that here we are using switches and the input type is radio. Also, you can see that the first Radio switch has the checked name attribute and the second radio switch has the name attribute (meaning the first switch is the active one).

We have also used the .small class in tandem with the .switch class resulting in the size being small compared to the default one.

The output of the code on execution is displayed in Figure 4-19.

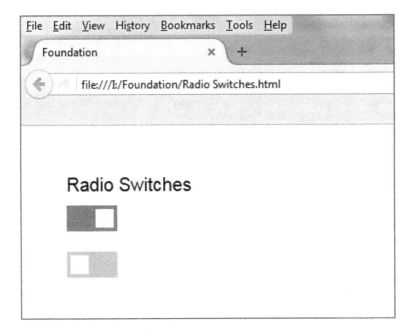

Figure 4-19. Radio Switches

From Figure 4-19, you can see that the first switch is active, whereas the other one is off. If you turn off the first switch, then the second one would become active.

Forms

Forms are a useful resource to allow users to enter data and to enable this collected data to be sent to servers for processing purposes. Foundation's Forms components are versatile and easy-to-code. You can use the built-in grid layout and define the responsive classes such as .large-7 or .small-9 to determine the size of fields on devices of different sizes. With the concept of displaying email addresses on the website becoming outdated due to phishing or spam bulk mails, contacts forms are trendy. We will understand the procedure of building forms in an easy-to-follow step-by-step method so that you get the concepts right.

Everything in the form must be included between the <form> tags. We first create a <form> opening and closing tag. Then, we create a <div> with the .row class and within that <div>, we create another <div> and assign the .small-6 columns class to it so that it spans across 6 virtual columns. We then create a <label> and then assign the input type as email. The code is displayed as follows:

```
<form>
    <div class="row">
        <div class="small-6 columns">
            <label>Email
            <input type="email" id="inputEmail" placeholder="Email">
        </label>
            </div>
</div>
</form>
```

Similarly, we create the Password section using the following code snippet:

```
<div class="row">
        <div class="small-6 columns">
            <label for="inputPassword">Password
            <input type="password" id="inputPassword" placeholder="Password">
                    </label>
        </div>
```

Here the code is almost similar to the Email one, but the input type used for the Password textbox is password. Remember all the code has to be included between the <form> tags.

We move on to create a button and here the button type would be submit which is the norm if you are creating a button inside a form.

```
<div class="row">
                <div class= "small-2 columns">
        <button class="button" type="submit">Login</button>
</div>
</div>
```

As you can see, we have assigned the button type as submit and assigned the button name as Login.

The entire code snippet is displayed in Listing 4-18:

Listing 4-18.

```
<form>
      <div class="row">
            <div class="small-6 columns">
         <label>Email
         <input type="email" id="inputEmail" placeholder="Email">
                  </label>
      </div>
            </div>
            <div class="row">
      <div class="small-6 columns">
          <label for="inputPassword">Password
          <input type="password" id="inputPassword" placeholder="Password">
                  </label>
          </div>
            </div>
            <div class="row">
            <div class= "small-2 columns">
      <button class="button" type="submit">Login</button>
            </div>
            </div>
</form>
```

The output of this code on execution is displayed in Figure 4-20.

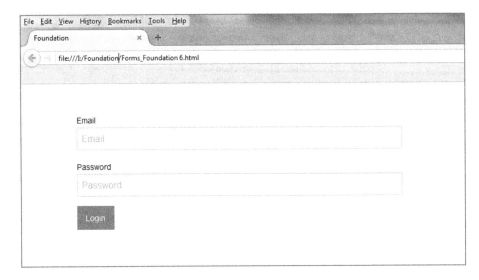

Figure 4-20. *Login Form*

One important thing to note is that Foundation supports a bunch of input types, namely- url, password, email, search, time, week, and month to mention a few.

Next, in the same form, we create a Search textbox. First create the row, as mentioned earlier, using the .row class. Create a <div> element within it and assign the .small-5 columns class to it. Then we create a <div> element and assign the .input-group class to it. The .input-group class is used when you want to combine text or allocate controls to the left or right of an input field. Basically, it is used as a wrapper. Then, we define the .input-group-field class to the input and assign the type as search. Then we create another <div> below the input tag and assign the .input-group-button class to it and define the button input type as submit and assign the value as Search.

After adding this inline input group to the existing code, the code snippet will look as displayed in Listing 4-19.

Listing 4-19.

```
<form>
        <div class="row">
                <div class="small-6 columns">
            <label>Email
            <input type="email" id="inputEmail" placeholder="Email">
                        </label>
        </div>
                </div>
                <div class="row">
        <div class="small-6 columns">
            <label for="inputPassword">Password
            <input type="password" id="inputPassword" placeholder="Password">
                        </label>
            </div>
                </div>
                <div class="row">
                <div class= "small-2 columns">
        <button class="button" type="submit">Login</button>
                </div>
                </div>
                <div class="row">
                <div class="small-5 columns">
                <div class="input-group">
        <input class="input-group-field" type="search">
                <div class="input-group-button">
                <input type="submit" class="button" value="Search">
                </div>
                </div>
                </div>
                </div>
</form>
```

The output of the code will be as displayed in Figure 4-21.

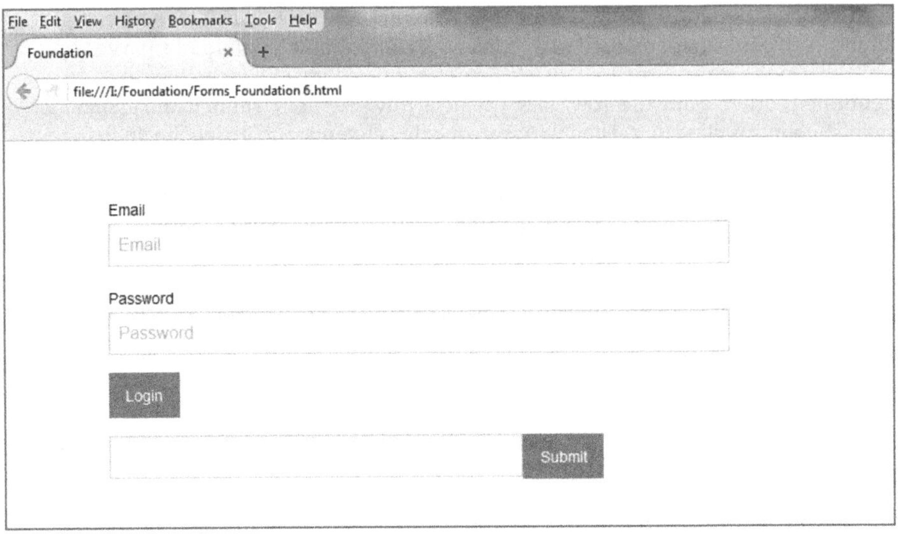

Figure 4-21. *Adding the Search textbox*

Next, we will take a look at the Fieldset attribute. Fieldsets are used to group similar or related elements in a form. They account for clean coding and enhance the degree of clarity of the form significantly. So, we will first create a row for the fieldset. Then we will use the fieldset tag and assign the .large-6 columns class to define the virtual span of the container. To the same .large-6 columns class, we will add a .fieldset class which will define the fieldset styles. Then we create a <label> and use two inputs and assign the text and placeholders. Then we create another <label> and using the <select> and <option> to create a dropdown list. We then close the label and define a button with the type as submit. Then we close the <fieldset> tag.

The code snippet for the entire page is displayed in Listing 4-20:

Listing 4-20.

```
<form>
      <div class="row">
              <div class="small-6 columns">
          <label>Email
          <input type="email" id="inputEmail" placeholder="Email">
                    </label>
      </div>
              </div>
              <div class="row">
      <div class="small-6 columns">
          <label for="inputPassword">Password
          <input type="password" id="inputPassword" placeholder="Password">
                    </label>
```

```
            </div>
                </div>
                <div class="row">
                <div class= "small-2 columns">
        <button class="button" type="submit">Login</button>
                </div>
                </div>
                <div class="row">
                <div class="small-5 columns">
                <div class="input-group">
        <input class="input-group-field" type="search">
                <div class="input-group-button">
                <input type="submit" class="button" value="Search">
                </div>
                </div>
                </div>
                </div>
        <div class="row">
    <fieldset class="large-6 columns fieldset">
    <legend>Personal Info</legend>
    <label> Enter Details Below
        <input type="text" placeholder="Enter Name">
            <input type="text" placeholder="Enter Address">
            <label> State
            <select>
            <option value="us1">New York</option>
            <option value="us2">California</option>
            <option value="us3">Florida</option>
            <option value="us4">Arizona</option>
                    <option value="us5">Texas</option>
            <option value="us6">Maine</option>
            <option value="us7">Ohio</option>
            </select>
            </label>
                <br>
                <button class="button" type="submit">Submit</button>
    </label>
</fieldset>
        </form>
```

The output of the code on execution is displayed in Figure 4-22.

Figure 4-22. *Form with the Fieldset*

Now suppose you want the labels for a field to the left of the input meaning it should be inline. It is very much possible in Foundation 6. Let's understand this by taking a look at the following code example. Refer to Listing 4-21 to see the code snippet.

Initially, we create a row and then create a <div> inside it and assign the .small 3 columns class to it. Then we create the label and assign the .text-right class to it. For alignment, we use the .middle class in conjunction with the .text-right class. Then we create another <div> and assign the .small-9 columns class to it. In that div, we assign email as the input type and enter a placeholder for it. Then we assign an id to the input tag and this id will be referenced with the for attribute of the <label>.

Remember, all this code for creating an inline label must be within that row.

Create another row after the previous row and paste the code. However, we will change the input type as password and the label name as Password in addition to changing the id for the second snippet.

If you have not already done so, refer to Listing 4-21 to see the code snippet for the explanation of inline labels:

Listing 4-21.

```
<form>
  <div class="row">
    <div class="small-3 columns">
      <label for="middle-label" class="text-right middle">Email</label>
    </div>
    <div class="small-9 columns">
      <input type="email" id="middle-label" placeholder="Enter Email address">
    </div>
  </div>
  <div class="row">
    <div class="small-3 columns">
      <label for="middle-label2" class="text-right middle">Password</label>
    </div>
    <div class="small-9 columns">
      <input type="password" id="middle-label2" placeholder="Enter password here">
      <p class="help-text">Your password must have special characters </p>
    </div>
  </div>
</form>
```

In Listing 4-21, you will see that we have added a <p> tag below the input for the password type and assigned a .help-text class to it. The .help-text class is used to give relevant and important information below the textbox. The output of the code will be as displayed in Figure 4-23.

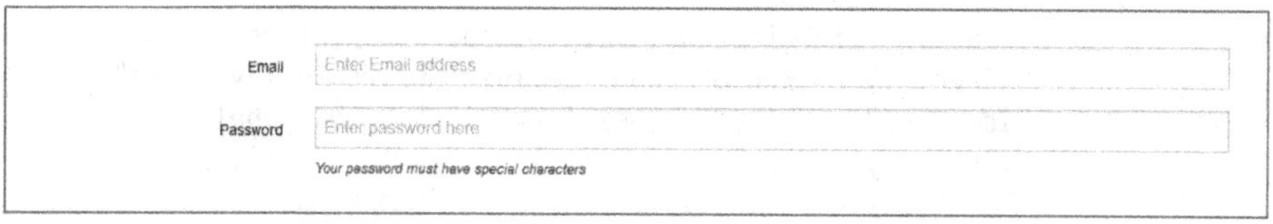

Figure 4-23. *Inline Labels*

Thereon, to add to the existing code, we add the Checkboxes and Radio buttons (as you do in normal HTML code). Then we create a button with the type as submit using the .button class.

Refer to Listing 4-22 to see the entire code snippet:

Listing 4-22.

```
<form>
  <div class="row">
    <div class="small-3 columns">
      <label for="middle-label" class="text-right middle">Email</label>
    </div>
    <div class="small-9 columns">
      <input type="email" id="middle-label" placeholder="Enter Email address">
    </div>
  </div>
  <form>
  <div class="row">
    <div class="small-3 columns">
      <label for="middle-label" class="text-right middle">Password</label>
    </div>
    <div class="small-9 columns">
      <input type="password" id="middle-label" placeholder=
      "Enter password here">
      <p class="help-text" id="passwordHelpText">Your password must have
      special characters </p>
        </div>
  </div>
  <br>
  <div class="row">
        <div class="small-6 columns">
                <label><ul> Select Delivery Method </ul></label>
                <input type="radio" name="deliver" value="deliverdine"
                id="Dine" required><label for="Dine">Dine</label>
                <input type="radio" name="deliver" value="delivercarryout"
                id="Carryout"><label for="Carryout">Carryout</label>
                <input type="radio" name="deliver" value="deliverhome"
                id="Delivery"><label for="Delivery">Delivery</label>
        </div>
        <div class="small-6 columns">
                <label> <ul> Product </ul></label>
                <input id="pizza" type="checkbox"><label for=
                "pizza">Pizza</label>
                <input id="burger" type="checkbox"><label
                for="burger">Burger</label>
                <input id="fish" type="checkbox"><label for="fish">Fish &
                Chips</label>
        </div>
```

```
        </div>
        <br>
            <div class="row">
                    <div class= "small-5 small-centered columns">
            <button class="button large success" type="submit">Order</button>
                    </div>
            </div>
</form>
```

The output of the code on execution is displayed in Figure 4-24.
Therefore, we now know how to create basic forms in Foundation 6.

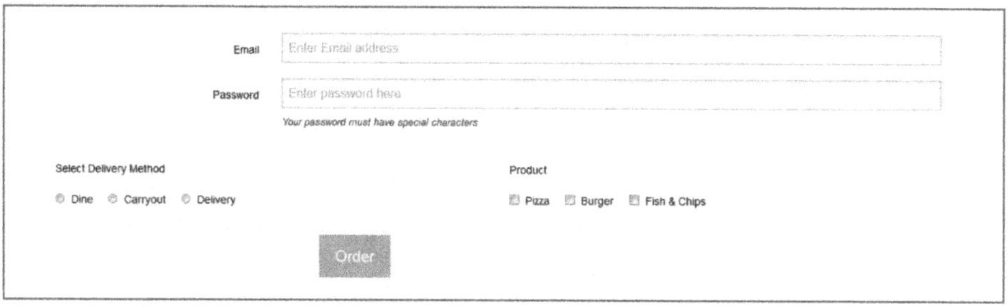

Figure 4-24. *Inline Form with Checkboxes and Radio Buttons*

Summary

In this chapter, we learned the various CSS utilities that you can implement while developing complex websites. Foundation's CSS Components make your web designing tasks much easier as you do not have to write code from scratch. Foundation adheres to the DRY (Don't Repeat Yourself) principle as you do not have to rewrite code each time you work on a different web designing project. The common design elements are broken into components that you can reuse multiple times for different projects thereby resulting in clean and systematic coding. In the next chapter, we will take an in-depth look at the JavaScript utilities of Foundation such as Modals, ToolTips, Dropdowns, Accordion and Alerts which you can implement while developing interactive websites.

CHAPTER 5

▓ ▓ ▓

JavaScript Components

Foundation comes bundled with JavaScript components to add intricate functionality. The JavaScript components can be incorporated into your projects thereby making your front-end development faster and easier.

We will learn about the following JavaScript components in this chapter:

- Tabs

- Accordions

- Dropdowns

- Data-Interchange

- Equalizers

- Modals

- Tooltips

- Data Toggler

You can pass the settings to the plug-ins through the mark-up using data-options.

If you check the mark-up of all the coding examples so far in this book, you can see the following lines of code:

```
<script src="https://cdnjs.cloudflare.com/ajax/libs/foundation/6.0.1/js/
vendor/jquery.min.js"></script>
<script src="https://cdnjs.cloudflare.com/ajax/libs/foundation/6.0.1/js/
foundation.min.js"></script>
<script src="https://cdnjs.cloudflare.com/ajax/libs/foundation/6.0.1/js/
vendor/what-input.min.js"></script>
```

You can see that the Foundation JavaScript components depend on jQuery and therefore, the jQuery CDN link must be placed before the Foundation JavaScript CDN link.

You can also see the following code in at the bottom of the markup-- just above the <body> section:

```
<script>
    $(document).foundation();
    </script>
```

The preceding code is used to initialize all the JavaScript components on your page.

Tabs

Tabs are increasingly being used in web design as you can present your content in a compact way. It allows you to keep multiple documents in a single window. You can use tabs as a navigation widget to switch between content resulting in a systematic and clean layout. Foundation's baked-in Tab Component helps you do just that by just adding a few lines of code.

Initially, you need to create a list using the <ul> and <li> elements. In the unordered list, you need to assign the .tabs class to the <ul> tag along with assigning the data-tabs to it. Then we define an id for the <ul> tag. To each list item, you need to assign the .tabs-title class to define the tab headings. To make one of the tabs active, you need to use the .is-active class in conjunction with the .tabs-title class for that specific tab as is displayed in the second <li> element (Section 2 tab) in the following code snippet:

```
<ul class="tabs" data-tabs id="tab_component">
  <li class="tabs-title"><a href="#pub1">Section 1</a></li>
  <li class="tabs-title is-active"><a href="#pub2">Section 2</a></li>
  <li class="tabs-title"><a href="#pub3">Section 3</a></li>
  <li class="tabs-title"><a href="#pub4">Section 4</a></li>
</ul>
```

Next, we define the contents of those tabs. For that, we create a <div> element and assign the .tabs-content class to it. Then we use the data-tabs-content attribute in conjunction with the .tabs-content class and assign the value to it. The value assigned must be the id assigned to the <ul> tag which defined the tab headings earlier. Then, we create the content section by creating <div> elements within the parent <div>. We assign the .tabs-panel for each child <div>. The id assigned to the <div> containing the contents must be the value of the <href> attribute in the <li> tags where we defined the tab headings for each item. You can also use the .is-active class to the <div> whose content would be active on executing the code.

The entire code snippet is shown in Listing 5-1:

Listing 5-1.

```html
<ul class="tabs" data-tabs id="tab_component">
  <li class="tabs-title"><a href="#pub1">Section 1</a></li>
  <li class="tabs-title is-active"><a href="#pub2">Section 2</a></li>
  <li class="tabs-title"><a href="#pub3">Section 3</a></li>
  <li class="tabs-title"><a href="#pub4">Section 4</a></li>
</ul>
<div class="tabs-content" data-tabs-content="tab_component">
  <div class="tabs-panel" id="pub1">
    <p>Far far away, behind the word mountains, far from the countries
    Vokalia and Consonantia, there live the blind texts.</p>
  </div>
  <div class="tabs-panel is-active" id="pub2">
    <p> Separated they live in Bookmarksgrove right at the coast of the
    Semantics, a large language ocean.  </p>
  </div>
  <div class="tabs-panel" id="pub3">
    <p>A small river named Duden flows by their place and supplies it with
    the necessary regelialia.</p>
  </div>
  <div class="tabs-panel" id="pub4">
    <p>It is a paradisematic country, in which roasted parts of sentences
    fly into your mouth. </p>
  </div>
</div>
```

The output of the code on execution is displayed in Figure 5-1.

Figure 5-1. *Tabs component*

Suppose you want the tabs to be vertical instead of the default horizontal alignment. Apart from just aligning them vertically, we can also place the tab headings and tab content next to each other.

Initially, we create a <div> element and assign the .row and .collapse classes to it. All the relevant code for the tabs component must be within the main <divs> which we created.

Then we create container <div> element in which we will create an unordered list as in the previous example. We assign the .small-4 columns class to that <div> which encloses the unordered list. The code for the headings is the same as the one for a Horizontal tab with one exception, we will add the .vertical class in conjunction with the .tabs class.

85

Refer to the following code snippet to understand it better:

```
<div class="row collapse">
  <div class="small-4 columns">
 <ul class="tabs vertical" data-tabs id="tab_component">
  <li class="tabs-title"><a href="#pub1">Section 1</a></li>
  <li class="tabs-title is-active"><a href="#pub2">Section 2</a></li>
  <li class="tabs-title"><a href="#pub3">Section 3</a></li>
  <li class="tabs-title"><a href="#pub4">Section 4</a></li>
</ul>
</div>
</div>
```

Then, we create the container for the content section. (Remember the last <div> is for the top main <div> with the .row and .collapse classes within which the entire code should be enclosed). For the content section, initially, we create a <div> and assign the .small-8 columns class to it. Then within that container, we use the same code as in the Horizontal tabs examples with one exception. We use the .vertical class in conjunction with the .tabs-content class. The entire code snippet is shown in Listing 5-2.

Listing 5-2.

```
<div class="row collapse">
  <div class="small-4 columns">
 <ul class="tabs vertical" data-tabs id="tab_component">
  <li class="tabs-title"><a href="#pub1">Section 1</a></li>
  <li class="tabs-title is-active"><a href="#pub2">Section 2</a></li>
  <li class="tabs-title"><a href="#pub3">Section 3</a></li>
  <li class="tabs-title"><a href="#pub4">Section 4</a></li>
</ul>
</div>
<div class="small-8 columns">
<div class="tabs-content vertical" data-tabs-content="tab_component">
  <div class="tabs-panel" id="pub1">
    <p>Far far away, behind the word mountains, far from the countries ,
    there live the blind texts. </p>
  </div>
  <div class="tabs-panel is-active" id="pub2">
    <p>Separated they live in Bookmarksgrove right at the coast of the
    Semantics, a  language ocean.</p>
  </div>
  <div class="tabs-panel" id="pub3">
    <p> A small river named Duden flows by their place and supplies it with
    the necessary products. </p>
  </div>
```

```
<div class="tabs-panel" id="pub4">
    <p> It is an awesome country, in which roasted parts of sentences fly
    into your mouth.    </p>
  </div>
</div>
 </div>
 </div>
```

On executing the code, the output is displayed in Figure 5-2.

Figure 5-2. *Vertical Tabs*

Accordions

Foundation's Accordion helps you encapsulate large amount of content in a compact area. They are similar to the Tabs plug-in where the menu-items collapse when you click on a new panel. The Accordions are styled like a stack of collapsible panels and act like a multi-level menu.

Let's understand the process of implementing the Accordion feature in Foundation. Initially we define the container grid for the Accordion using the .row and responsive classes:

```
<div class="row">
<div class = "small-8 small-centered columns">
</div>
</div>
```

Then we create a list and assign the .accordion class to <ul> tag. We also use the data-accordion and role attributes in tandem with the .accordion class. Thereon, we assign the tablist value to the role attribute.

Now we will create the headings and content for the first Accordion item. All the list items must be enclosed within the <ul> tags. We assign the .accordion-item class to the first <li> tag. Since we want this as the current active item, we assign an is-active class to it. Then, we define the name of the panel within the anchor <a> tags. We use the role attribute in the <a> tag and assign the tab value to it. We also define the title of that Accordion item using .the accordion-title class. Then we create a <div> element and assign an id to it which is incidentally the value of the href attribute for the preceding

87

anchor <a> tags. For the <div> element, we also allocate the .accordion-content class and the role attribute in addition to assigning the tabpanel value to the role attribute. Finally, we add the data-tab-content attribute to the <div> element for that list item.

We create two more list items as explained earlier and the entire code snippet is shown in Listing 5-3.

Listing 5-3. <div class="row">

```
<div class = "small-8 small-centered columns">
<ul class="accordion" data-accordion role="tablist">
<li class="accordion-item is-active">
  <a href="#section1 role="tab" class="accordion-title">About Apress Media LLC</a>
  <div id="section1" class="accordion-content"role="tabpanel"
  data-tab-content>
      Apress Media LLC provides high-quality content building a
      pathway to career success.
  </div>
</li>
<li class="accordion-item">
  <a href="#section2" role="tab" class="accordion-title">Apress News</a>
  <div id="section2" class="accordion-content"role="tabpanel"
  data-tab-content>
    Apress Media LLC is a technical publisher devoted to meeting
    the needs of IT professionals.
  </div>
</li>
<li class="accordion-item">
  <a href="#section3" role="tab" class="accordion-title">Apress
  Sales and Distribution</a>
  <div id="section3" class="accordion-content"role="tabpanel"
  data-tab-content>
    Apress titles are available to purchase just about everywhere
    in the World.
  </div>
</li>
</ul>
  </div>
</div>
```

The output of the code on execution is displayed in Figure 5-3.

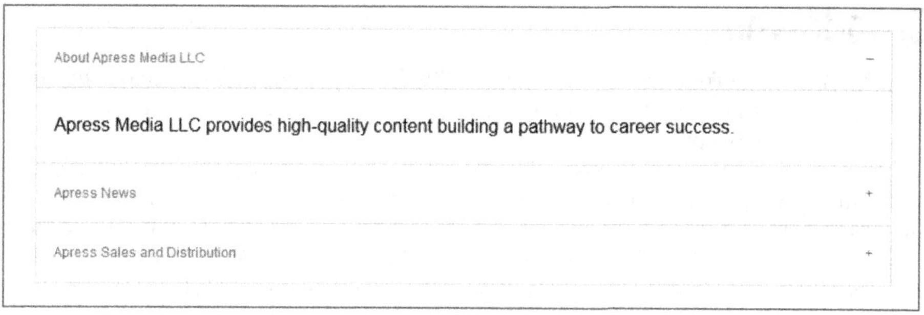

Figure 5-3. Accordion Component

Figure 5-3 displays the Accordion functionality and you can see the active panel displaying the content. If we click on any other panel, the default active panel is closed and the clicked panel will display the content.

However, if you want the content of multiple panels to be displayed without closing the panels which displayed their content, then we need to use the data-multi-expand="true" property with it. The data-multi-expand property allows multiple panels to be open with the content displayed provided you assign the value "true" to it.

The <ul> tag on adding the data-multi-expand property will look as follows:

```
<ul class="accordion" data-accordion role="tablist" data-multi-expand="true">
```

The output of the code in execution will display the panel and the content which is active and current. However, when you click on the second panel, the first panel is not closed.

Refer to Figure 5-4 to understand it better.

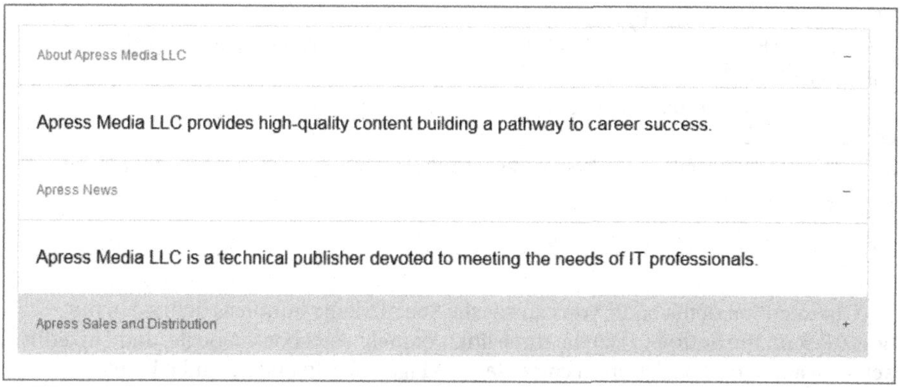

Figure 5-4. Multi-expanded Accordion panels

89

Dropdowns

Dropdown Panes in Foundation are a handy utility for displaying information on clicking or hovering over the element. In the following section, we will understand the procedure to create a Dropdown pane.

Initially, we will create a button using the <button> tag and assigning the .button class and type to it. We then use the data-toggle attribute in the same <button> tag. Then, we create a <div> element and assign the .dropdown-pane class to it. We use the id attribute and this assigned id will be referenced and linked as the value of the data-toggle attribute in the preceding <button> tag. We also the data-dropdown attribute and set the data-auto-focus attribute to true next to the id attribute in the same <div> element.

The code snippet for the earlier explanation for Dropdowns will be as follows:

```
<button class="button" type="button" data-toggle="example-dropdown">
Social Media</button>
<div class="dropdown-pane" id="example-dropdown" data-dropdown
data-auto-focus="true">
</div>
```

Then we define an unordered list between the <div> tags. In the unordered list, we use an inline style as list-style-type: none for the <ul> tag; the styling used will remove the bullets from the unordered list. We then create three list items between the <ul> tags. To the list items, we will use different background colors for more clarity.

The entire code snippet is shown in Listing 5-4:

Listing 5-4.

```
<button class="button" type="button" data-toggle="example-dropdown">Social
Media</button>
<div class="dropdown-pane" id="example-dropdown" data-dropdown data-auto-
focus="true">
<ul style="list-style-type:none">
 <li style="background: #00BFFF;"><a href="https://www.facebook.com/">
 Facebook</a></li>
 <li style="background: #F08080;"><a href="https://www.google.co.in">
 Google</a></li>
 <li style="background: #D3D3D3;"><a href="https://in.linkedin.com/">
 LinkedIn</a></li>
</ul>
</div>
```

On execution of the code, you can see the Social Media button as defined in the code. Click on the button to see the three links, namely- Facebook, Google, and LinkedIn each with a different background color. Refer to Figure 5-5 to understand it better.

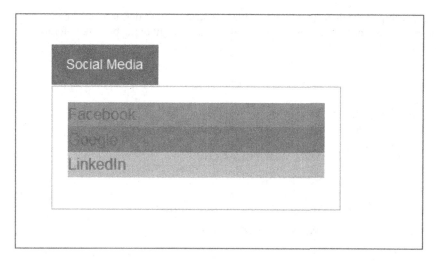

Figure 5-5. Dropdown pane

Suppose you want the Dropdown pane to be aligned to the right of the button instead of below the button. In that case, you can use the .right class in conjunction with the .dropdown-pane class in the <div> element which follows the <button> tag.

Also, if you want the dropdown list or content to be displayed on hovering over the element, you remove the data-auto-focus="true" property in the <div> and replace it with the data-hover="true", meaning you use the data-hover attribute and add the true value to it.

To show an example of the hover functionality and the alignment of the Dropdown pane to the right, we will create a button using the .button class assigned inside the <button> tag. Then we use the data-toggle attribute in the <button> element. Next, we define a <div> element with the .dropdown-pane class and use the .right class along with it in addition to the data-dropdown attribute. The .right class results in positioning the dropdown pane to the right.

Along with it, we use the data-hover attribute and assign the "true" value to it. As a result, you will see the dropdown pane if you just hover over the button. Then we define a callout panel with the .success class for a <div> within the earlier <div>.

Refer to Listing 5-5 to see the entire code snippet:

Listing 5-5.

```
<button class="button" type="button" data-toggle="example2"> Right Pane </
button>
<div class="dropdown-pane right" id="example2" data-dropdown data-
hover="true">
<div class=" success callout">
  <h5>You wanna know something! </h5>
  <p> Yeah! Crazy Jay bought many exquisite opal jewels.</p>
 </button>
</div>
</div>
```

On executing the code, you will see the Right Pane button as defined in the code. If you hover over the button, you will see the callout to the right of the button. Refer to Figure 5-6 to see how it works.

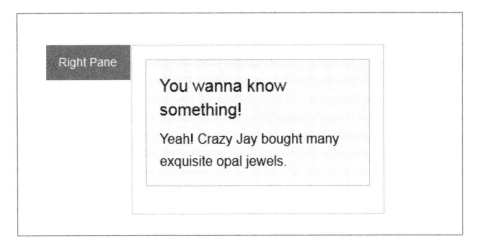

Figure 5-6. *Right aligned Dropdown pane on Hover*

Data-Interchange

Foundation's Data-Interchange plug-in is quite handy when it comes to images. Basically, this utility helps you load different content depending on the screen size. You can use light-weight content on mobile devices and robust heavy-duty content on medium-and-large-screen devices.

Let's understand this using an example. We create a <div> element and use the image <img> tag within it. We use the data-interchange attribute in the image <img> tag and define the image depending on the screen-size. Refer to Listing 5-6 to understand it better:

Listing 5-6.

```
<div>
 <img data-interchange="[http://placehold.it/220x200, small],
 [http://placehold.it/770x350, large]">
</div>
```

In Listing 5-6, we have defined the image placeholder for the small screen with a width of 220 and height of 200 for the small screen. For the large screen, we have used the image placeholder with dimensions of 770 as the width, and 350 as the height. (Note: We have use the http://placehold.it/ service for displaying the data-interchange attribute).

On execution of the code on a large screen, you will see the image placeholder with dimensions of 770*350 as displayed in Figure 5-7.

Figure 5-7. *Image on large screen*

On smaller screens, you can see the image with reduced dimensions of 220*200 as displayed in Figure 5-8 (you can also decrease the browser size to simulate a smaller screen).

Figure 5-8. *Image on small screens*

Therefore, you can see how handy this utility is when you want to load light-weight content on smaller screens and massive content on larger screens.

Equalizers

The size of panels differ depending on the content inside them. Foundation's Equalizer attribute helps maintain uniform height for different panels. You need to assign the data-equalizer attribute to the main container. Then apply the data-equalizer-watch attribute to the concerned panels resulting in equal height for all those panels. The data-equalizer-watch attribute helps inheriting the height of the tallest element.

Let's understand this using a code example. We will create three callout panels and define minimal amount of content for the first panel, increase the content in the second panel and end up using maximum content for the third panel. We create a row initially and assign the data-equalizer attribute in conjunction with the .row class.

We move on to defining the three callout panels. First we assign the responsive classes by assigning the .large-4 columns class for each panel and then create the three panels using the .callout class. We also assign the .warning class for more emphasis. We use the data-equalizer-watch attribute in conjunction with each .callout class.

Refer to Listing 5-7 to see the entire code snippet:

Listing 5-7.

```
<div class="row" data-equalizer>
  <div class="large-4 columns">
    <div class="callout warning" data-equalizer-watch>
      A small river named Duden flows by their place and supplies
      it with the necessary regalia.
    </div>
  </div>
  <div class="large-4 columns">
    <div class="callout warning" data-equalizer-watch>
      <p>A small river named Duden flows by their place and supplies
      it with the necessary regalia. The Big Oxmox advised her not to do so,
      because there were thousands of bad Commas, wild Question Marks and
      devious Semikoli, but the Little Blind Text didn't listen.</p>
    </div>
  </div>
  <div class="large-4 columns">
    <div class="callout warning" data-equalizer-watch>
      A small river named Duden flows by their place and supplies it with
      the necessary regalia. The Big Oxmox advised her not to do so, because
      there were thousands of bad Commas, wild Question Marks and devious
      Semikoli, but the Little Blind Text didn't listen. Even the all-
      powerful Pointing has no control about the blind texts it is an almost
      unorthographic life. One day however a small line of blind text by the
      name of Lorem Ipsum decided to leave for the far World of Grammar.
    </div>
  </div>
</div>
```

On executing the code, three panels with varying amount of content have equal height and are spaced evenly across the row. Refer to Figure 5-9 to see the output.

Figure 5-9. *Equalizer functionality*

Nesting is also possible in Data Equalizers. You can nest equalized elements within the parent container. In the following example, initially we create a <div> with the row class along with the data-equalizer attribute. We assign the value pub1 to the data-equalizer attribute. Then we create three callout panels each spanning a width of four columns across the row in addition to using the .success class to it. We have inherited the same value "pub1" for each of those callouts.

The code snippet for the explanation above is as follows:

```
<div class="row" data-equalizer="pub1">
 <div class="large-4 columns">
    <div class="callout success" data-equalizer-watch="pub1">
     <h3>Main Panel</h3>
                <p> It wasn't a dream </p>
       </div>
  </div>

<div class="large-4 columns">
    <div class="callout success" data-equalizer-watch="pub1">
     <h3>Main Panel</h3>
                <p> It wasn't a dream </p>
       </div>
  </div>
<div class="large-4 columns">
    <div class="callout success" data-equalizer-watch="pub1">
     <h3>Main Panel</h3>
                <p> It wasn't a dream </p>
       </div>
  </div>
 </div>
 </div>
```

On executing the code, you will see the three callout panels evenly spread across the row. Refer to Figure 5-10 to understand it better.

Figure 5-10. *Main panels evenly spread across the row*

Following this, we now nest three callout panels in the first Callout panel. Initially after the first paragraph element in the first callout, we create a row and assign the value "publish" for the data-equalizer attribute. Then we create three nested callouts each and assign the warning contextual class along for them. Then, we assign the data-equalizer-watch attribute in conjunction with the .callout class for each callout panel and assign the value "publish" to the data-equalizer-watch attributes. The complete code snippet for the code example is shown in Listing 5-8:

Listing 5-8.

```
<div class="row" data-equalizer="pub1">
  <div class="large-4 columns">
    <div class=" callout success" data-equalizer-watch="pub1">
    <h3>Main Panel </h3>
        <p>It wasn't a dream</p>
    <div class="row" data-equalizer="publish">
      <div class="callout warning" data-equalizer-watch="publish">
        <h5>Nested Panel 1</h5>
                <p> Travelling day in and day out.  </p>
      </div>
      <div class="callout warning" data-equalizer-watch="publish">
        <h5>Nested Panel 2 </h5>
                <p> Travelling day in and day out.. </p>
      </div>
      <div class="callout warning" data-equalizer-watch="publish">
        <h5>Nested Panel 3</h5>
                <p> Travelling day in and day out. </p>
      </div>
    </div>
    </div>
  </div>
</div>
```

```
<div class="large-4 columns">
  <div class="callout success" data-equalizer-watch="pub1">
    <h3>Main Panel</h3>
            <p> It wasn't a dream </p>
      </div>
  </div>
<div class="large-4 columns">
    <div class="callout success" data-equalizer-watch="pub1">
    <h3>Main Panel</h3>
            <p> It wasn't a dream </p>
      </div>
  </div>
</div>
```

On executing the code, we will see the output where three nested callout panels are enclosed in the first callout panel. Also the second and third main callout panels have automatically inherited the enhanced heights of the first main callout Panel containing those three nested callout panels. Refer to Figure 5-11 to see the output of the executed code.

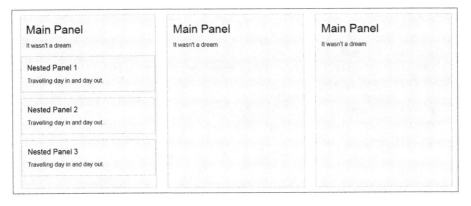

Figure 5-11. *Nested Equalizers*

Modals

Modals help you overlay an element over your website. A modal is generally used as an alternative to conventional pop-ups. You can literally see the information without leaving the page you are viewing. It also counts for awesome aesthetics and is a resourceful utility that significantly enhances usability. In Foundation, you can design modals with minimalistic amount of markup.

Let's understand the procedure to create a basic Modal. Create an anchor <a> tag and assign a .button class to it. Then next to the .button class, add a data-open attribute and assign a value to it. The data-open attribute is the one that fires the modal.

```
<a href="#" class="button" data-open="pub1"> Modal button </a>
```

Next, create a container element, in this case a <div>. Create an id for the <div>. The id created must be the same one that is referenced by the data-open attribute in the anchor tag defined earlier. To the same <div>, add the .reveal class and the data-reveal attribute. Add the content that is to be displayed in the pop-up. Then we move on to create a Close button. The Close button is created by using a <button> tag to which we assign the .close-button class. We assign the type as button and also use the data-close attribute in the same <button> tag. We then add the aria-label attribute and assign the "Close reveal value" to it. Then we create an inline <span> element and use the × unicode and then close the <span> tag followed by closing the <button> tag. The entire code snippet for the Modal feature is shown in Listing 5-9:

Listing 5-9.

```
<a href="#" class="button" data-open="pub1"> Modal button </a>
 <div id="pub1" class="reveal" data-reveal>
   <h3>Hey You</h3>
   <p><strong> Is there anybody out there </strong></p>
   <p> Goodness! It is eerie when there is absolute silence </p>
  <button class="close-button" aria-label="Close reveal" type="button">
    <span aria-hidden="true">&times;</span>
  </button>
 </div>
```

On executing the code, you can see the button called Modal Button as defined in the code. On clicking it, the modal will pop-up on top of the page. Refer to Figure 5-12 to understand it better:

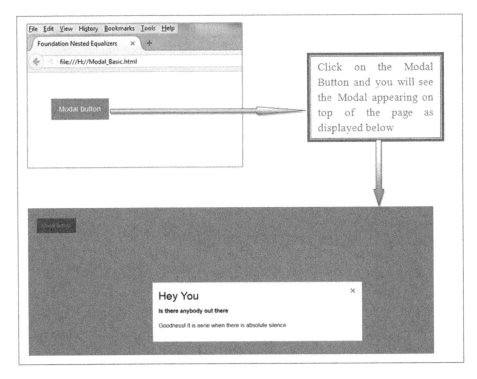

Figure 5-12. *Basic Modal example*

You can nest a Modal within another Modal. Let's understand the procedure to create a nested modal in the following code example. Initially, we create a button using the .button class in an anchor <a> tag. Use the data-toggle attribute and assign a value to it, which is the same as the id assigned to the container <div> element that follows the <a> tag. Assign the .reveal class to the container <div> element. Add the content you will be using in the first modal.

The code snippet so far looks as follows:

```
<a href="#" data-toggle="pub1" class="button ">Wall</a>
<!-- Reveal Modals begin -->
<div id="pub1" class="reveal" data-reveal>
  <h3 id="pub1Title"> Hey You.</h3>
  <p>Is there anybody out there</p>
```

After this, we immediately create the button for the second modal. We assign the .success class in conjunction with the .button class and assign a value to the data-toggle attribute used alongside it. Then we create a close button similar to the code used in the basic modal example. We close the <div> and then we proceed to create the content for the second modal.

Create another <div> element to which we assign the reveal class and then use similar code to create the content of the second modal. The id for the <div> element will be the referenced by the data-toggle attribute for the button created earlier for the second modal. We move on to add the content and then create a close button for the second modal.

The entire code snippet is shown in Listing 5-10:

Listing 5-10.

```
<a href="#" data-toggle="pub1" class="button ">Wall</a>
<!-- Reveal Modals begin -->
<div id="pub1" class="reveal" data-reveal>
  <h3 id="pub1Title"> Hey You.</h3>
  <p>Is there anybody out there</p>
  <p><a href="#" data-toggle="pub2" class="success button">Echoes</a></p>
  <button class="close-button" data-close aria-label="Close reveal" type="button">
    <span aria-hidden="true">&times;</span>
  </button>
</div>

<div id="pub2" class="reveal" data-reveal>
  <h3 id="pub2Title"> Dream On </h3>
  <p>Hey Joe, in the end, it doesn't matter which side you are on</p>
  <p>In the end, it is just the end. Music's over, Turn off the lights! <p>
    <button class="close-button" data-close aria-label="Close reveal" type="button">
    <span aria-hidden="true">&times;</span>
  </button>
</div>
```

The output of the code will result in a button called Wall as defined in the code as shown if Figure 5-13.

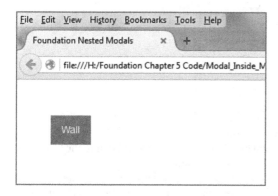

Figure 5-13. *Button for the first modal*

Click on this button and the first modal appears on top of the page. On clicking the Echoes button, the second modal is fired replacing the first modal. We have shown the procedure using Figure 5-14 where we have taken close-ups snaps of the output.

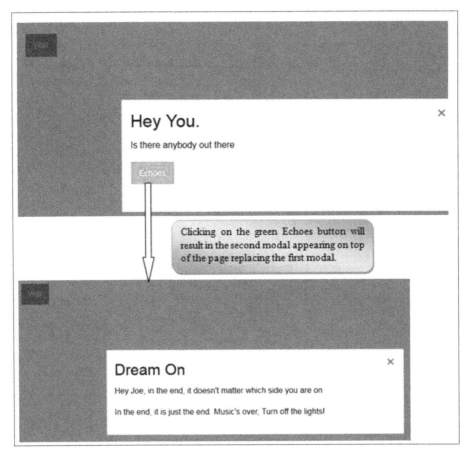

Figure 5-14. Modal inside a modal

ToolTips

Tooltips are labels that are displayed on hovering over an element.

Let's understand by means of a simple example. Create a row and define the responsive class and the width and position of the container.

Moving forward, create an element and assign a .has-tip class to it. Apply the data-tooltip attribute in conjunction with the .has-tip class. Enter the title which will be displayed as the tool tip upon hovering over the content. Also use the data-disable-hover attribute and assign the value "false" to it.

Refer to the code snippet for the tool-tip as defined in Listing 5-11.

Listing 5-11.

```
<div class="row">
   <div class = "small-8 small-centered columns">
   <div data-tooltip class="has-tip" data-disable-hover='false' title="
Foundation"> Mobile-First Framework </div>
</div>
```

Refer to Figure 5-15 to see the output of the executed code.

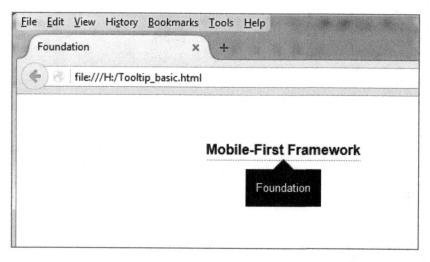

Figure 5-15. *Basic Tooltip*

On hover, you can see the tool-tip as displayed in Figure 5-15.

You can also change the alignment of the tooltip to the top, right or left by using the .top, .right and .left classes respectively in conjunction with the .has-tip class.

We will look at the following code snippet in Listing 5-12 to understand the procedure of aligning the tooltip to the left.

Listing 5-12.

```
<div class="row">
   <div class = "small-8 small-centered columns">
         <div data-tooltip class="has-tip left" data-disable-hover='false'
         title="Foundation - To the left">Awesome Framework </div>
      </div>
</div>
```

The output of the code will result in a tooltip aligned to the left as displayed in Figure 5-16.

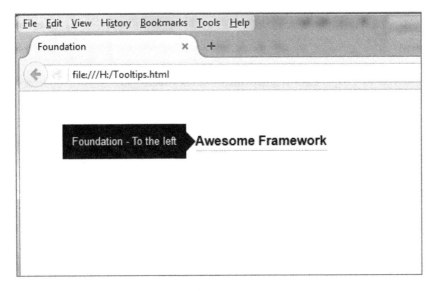

Figure 5-16. *Left aligned Tooltip*

Data-Toggler

The Data-Toggler attribute helps you toggle CSS or animate an element just by a click. We will take a look at a code example to see how it works at a basic level. Initially, we create a list of items using the <ul> tag. Refer to Listing 5-13 to see the code for the Data-Toggler feature:

Listing 5-13.

```
<ul class="menu" id="pub" data-toggler=".expanded">
  <li><a href="#">John</a></li>
  <li><a href="#">Jack</a></li>
  <li><a href="#">Jill</a></li>
  <li><a href="#">Janet</a></li>
  <li><a href="#">Jonas</a></li>
</ul>
<br>
<button class="button" type="button"  data-toggle="pub">Click to Expand</button>
```

Initially, we create a list of items using the <ul> and its nested <li> tags. To the <ul> tag, we assign an id and the data-toggler attribute. We assign the .expanded class to the data-toggler attribute. In this example, we want to toggle the .expanded class. (You need to assign the class you want to toggle to the data-toggler attribute). We move on to defining a button which on clicking will toggle the .expanded class. Create a button using the <button> tag and use the data-toggle attribute to it. To the data-toggle attribute, we assign the value of the id of the <ul> tag.

The output on executing the code is shown in Figure 5-17.

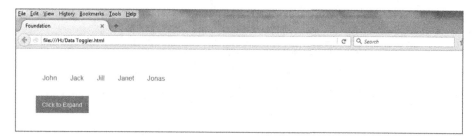

Figure 5-17. *Initial Code output for the Data Toggle feature*

Now if you click on the Click to Expand button on the screen, the names in the output (as defined in the list items in the code) will expand and extend evenly on the same row.

Refer to Figure 5-18 to see the expanded action on clicking the button.

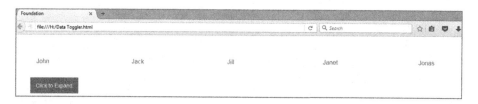

Figure 5-18. *Expanded Toggle functionality*

Summary

In this chapter, we explored most of the JavaScript add-ons and plug-ins in Foundation. The functionalities and features were explained using just the data attributes-- minimizing the use of writing vanilla JavaScript code. The jQuery components adhere to the Write Less and Do More paradigm resulting in clean and lean coding. In the next chapter, we will take a look at Foundation with Sass at a very basic level to understand how it works.

■ ■ ■

Intro to Foundation with Sass

Foundation's CSS and JavaScript components make web designing a breeze. However, there are times when the bloat and bulk of the CSS file is huge due to the complexity of the project. Also, there are times when the websites developed using Foundation or any other CSS framework look similar due to the common features used. Add to it the time and effort that you would need to deliver as per the deadlines.

Enter Sass: a CSS pre-processor with a whole bunch of goodies such as nesting rules, variables, and mixins to mention a few. Foundation with Sass helps you create intricate projects in half the time without the normal clutter. In this chapter, we will discuss the installation procedure of Sass and a simple example of how it can change the way you code in Foundation.

Getting started with Foundation with SaaS

We will now install the Sass version of Foundation on the Windows operating system. The easiest way to do so is by using the Command Line interface or what you call Command Prompt in Windows.

Well there are pre-requisites prior to installation, namely –

```
Git
Node.js
```

Git, a distributed version control system can be downloaded from the following website:

```
http://git-scm.com/
```

Since we are using Windows, you need to download the relevant file (compatible with your versions of Windows, be it 32-bit or 64-bit) on the website.

A couple of points are important if you are installing Git on Windows. As you click on the installer, you will come across the following window after a few steps (Refer Figure 6-1).

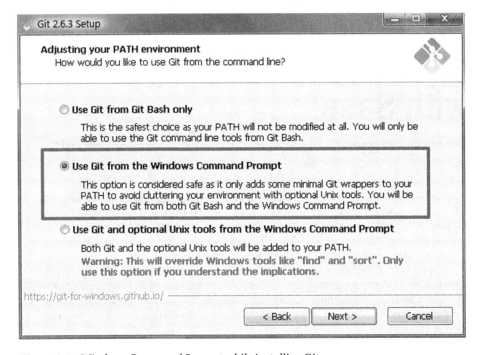

Figure 6-1. *Windows Command Prompt while installing Git*

Make sure that you are using the Windows Command Prompt option which is highlighted in a red box in the preceding screenshot.

Complete the Git installation by choosing the appropriate options in the setup. Ensure that the path of the Environment Variables as well as the System variables have been configured correctly.

Next, you need to set up Node.js and install it. Node.js is power packed with Build tools and helps you run JavaScript outside the browser.

You can download Node from the following link:

```
https://nodejs.org/en/
```

Click on the downloaded Node installer and ensure that the path of the Environment and System Variables are configured correctly. This is essential as you will not be able to use Foundation Sass if it is not configured correctly.

Now that we have installed the pre-requisites, we can move on to the Command Prompt.

Go to the command prompt and type in the following command.

```
npm install --global foundation-cli
```

Refer to Figure 6-2 to understand it better.

Figure 6-2. Installing Foundation CLI

Once you run the command, the Foundation CLI will be installed.
Once CLI is installed, let's create a project.
The following command should be run in the Command Prompt window:

```
foundation new
```

On running the command, you will be prompted to choose one among the three options as displayed in Figure 6-3.

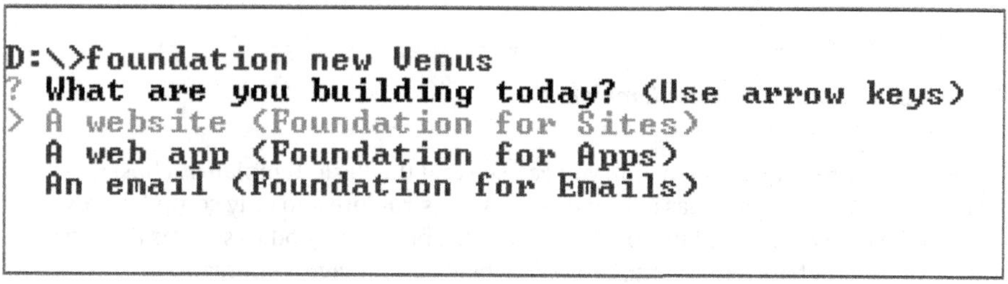

Figure 6-3. Choosing Foundation for Sites option

From the preceding screenshot, you can see the Foundation for Sites selected as the default option. As you can see, Foundation for Apps and Foundation for Emails are the other two options.

We will choose the default Foundation for Sites from the list. Press Enter and you will be prompted for the project name. We will enter Venus as the project name (you can use any project name, in this example, we are creating a project called Venus).

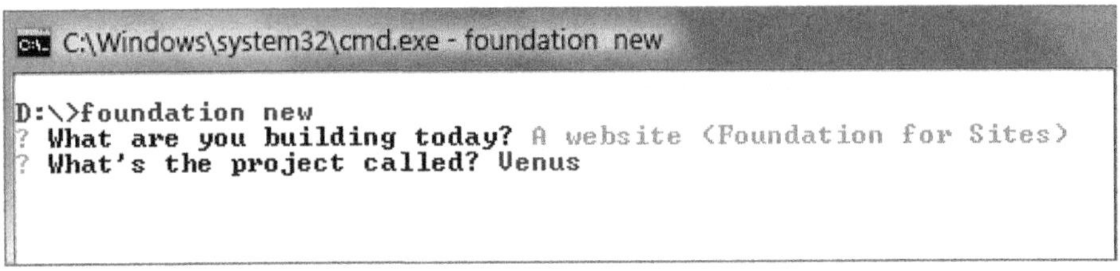

Figure 6-4. *Creating a project*

Once you enter the project name and Press Enter, you will need to choose from the following two options:

Basic Template

ZURB Template

Refer to Figure 6-5 to understand it better.

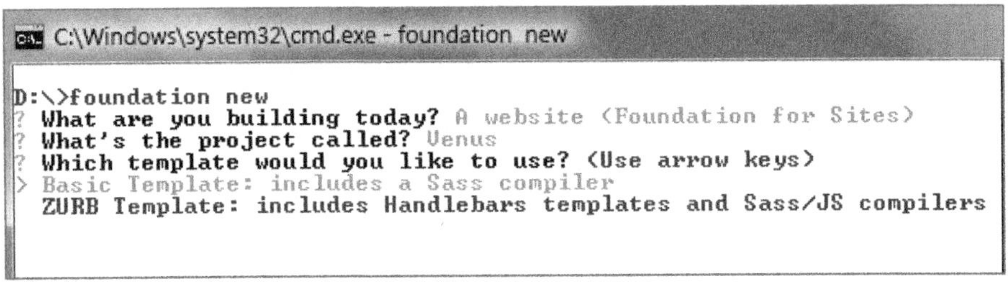

Figure 6-5. *Choosing the Basic Template*

From the preceding screenshot, you can see that the Basic Template is chosen by default. The Basic template has a fixed directory file structure and only compiles only Sass whereas the Zurb template comes along with a bunch of goodies such as Processing JavaScript, Handlebars templating, Browser Syncing and Image compression.

We will choose the Basic Template in this example. On choosing the basic template, it will download the project template along with installing all the dependencies. Then it will ask you to go to the project folder and run the following command as shown in Figure 6-6.

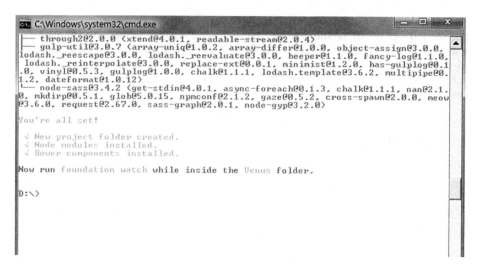

Figure 6-6. *Screen post installation*

Go to the Project folder (in this case, Venus). Type in the following command:

```
foundation watch
```

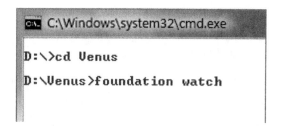

Figure 6-7. *Running Foundation watch to compile Sass for the first time*

After you run the command, you can see that the project template is created. Foundation uses the Gulp build tool for compiling the Sass files. (In the Zurb template, It also helps in tasks such as compressing the Sass and js files, copying modified files to the output directory, and refreshing the browser on the go to mention a few). On compilation, you can go to the Venus Project folder using Windows explorer and you can see the following file structure:

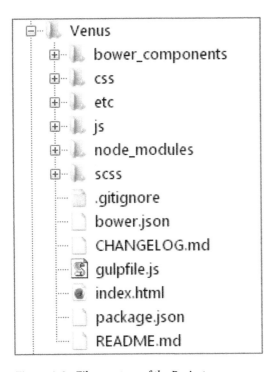

Figure 6-8. *File structure of the Project*

Let's shed some light over some of these files, namely - the app.js file in the js folder, _settings.scss and app.scss file in the scss folder and app.css in the stylesheets folder.

app.js

This is where we initialize the JavaScript add-ons and plug-ins. You can also add custom JavaScript in this file to enhance the functionality.

_settings.scss

This file contains Foundation's Sass variables and you have the facility of modifying this file to customize your Foundation version. The _settings.scss file is a child of the app.scss file listed below.

app.scss

In this file, all the Foundation components and styles are imported. However, you can be selective by importing only those utilities that are required by deactivating the components you do not need and selecting the ones which are essential. You can also write or import custom Sass here.

app.css

On compiling the SCSS files, the output CSS files are saved here. Remember that if you make any changes in this file, and then compile the SCSS files, then the mix-up will override the CSS files here. Therefore, you can include the custom CSS styles in the SCSS files itself so that it will be compiled to files here.

The basic HTML markup for a new file (when you are creating a new HTML file and not the default one) is as displayed in Listing 6-1.

Listing 6-1. Basic Markup

```
<!doctype html>
<html class="no-js" lang="en">
<head>
<meta charset="utf-8">
<meta http-equiv="x-ua-compatible" content="ie=edge">
<meta name="viewport" content="width=device-width, initial-scale=1.0">
<title>Foundation for Sites</title>
<link rel="stylesheet" href="css/app.css">
</head>
<body>

<script src="bower_components/jquery/dist/jquery.js"></script>
<script src="bower_components/what-input/what-input.js"></script>
<script src="bower_components/foundation-sites/dist/foundation.js"></script>
<script src="js/app.js"></script>
</body>
</html>
```

Let's create a callout and assign the secondary color to it. The code will look as defined in Listing 6-2.

Listing 6-2. Adding a callout

```
<!doctype html>
<html class="no-js" lang="en">
<head>
<meta charset="utf-8">
<meta http-equiv="x-ua-compatible" content="ie=edge">
<meta name="viewport" content="width=device-width, initial-scale=1.0">
<title>Foundation for Sites</title>
<link rel="stylesheet" href="css/app.css">
</head>
<body>
<div class="row">
        <div class="small-8 small-centered columns">
        <h3>This is a secondary panel</h3>
<div class="callout secondary">
    Far far away, behind the word mountains, far from the countries Vokalia
    and Consonantia, there live the blind texts. Separated they live in
    Bookmarksgrove right at the coast of the Semantics, a large language
    ocean.
<div>
        </div>
        </div>
<script src="bower_components/jquery/dist/jquery.js"></script>
<script src="bower_components/what-input/what-input.js"></script>
<script src="bower_components/foundation-sites/dist/foundation.js"></script>
<script src="js/app.js"></script>
</body>
</html>
```

The output of the code on execution will be as displayed in Figure 6-9.

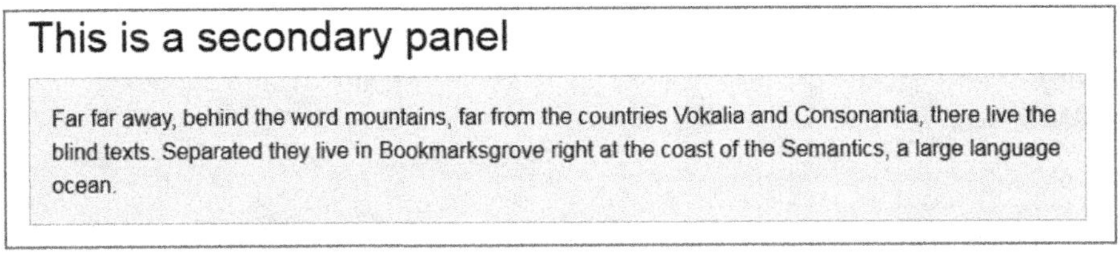

This is a secondary panel

Far far away, behind the word mountains, far from the countries Vokalia and Consonantia, there live the blind texts. Separated they live in Bookmarksgrove right at the coast of the Semantics, a large language ocean.

Figure 6-9. *Secondary callout*

The next step is to make changes in the SCSS files. Remember that custom CSS and SCSS must be a part of the app.scss file. If you want to make changes in your Foundation version, then you can change it in the _settings.scss file which in turn is a child of the app. scss file. What it means is that things you cannot do or implement in the _settings.scss file can be done in the app.scss file. As explained earlier, you can be selective and only choose those components that you require in the app.scss file.

The global value for secondary-color is defined as #777 as defined in Figure 6-10.

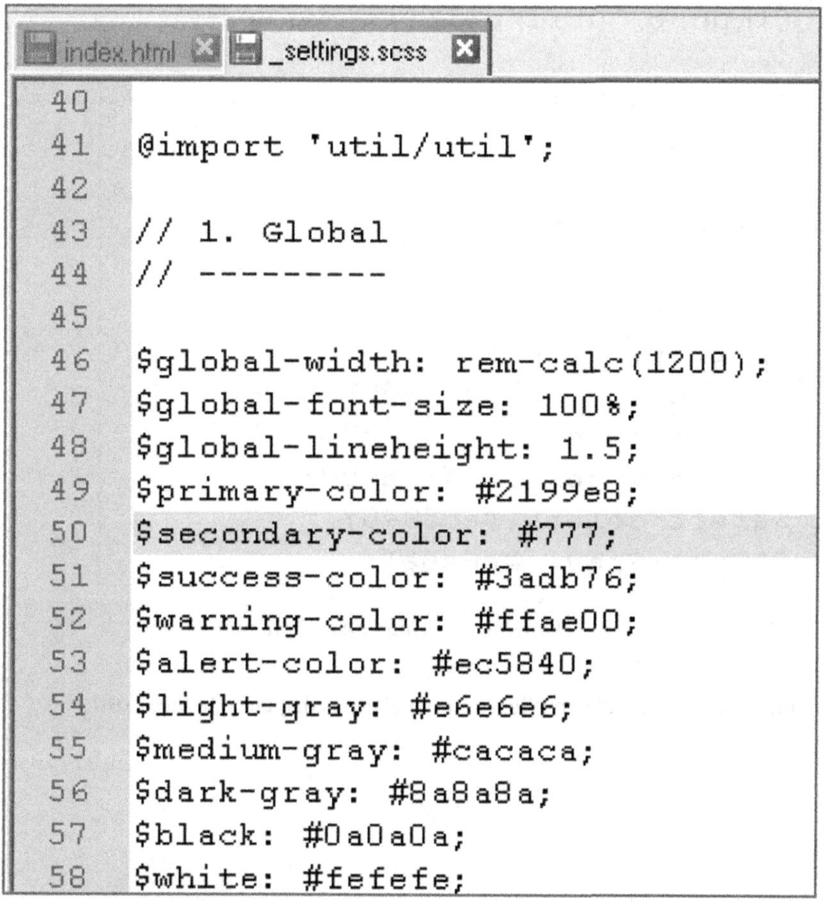

```scss
40
41    @import 'util/util';
42
43    // 1. Global
44    // ---------
45
46    $global-width: rem-calc(1200);
47    $global-font-size: 100%;
48    $global-lineheight: 1.5;
49    $primary-color: #2199e8;
50    $secondary-color: #777;
51    $success-color: #3adb76;
52    $warning-color: #ffae00;
53    $alert-color: #ec5840;
54    $light-gray: #e6e6e6;
55    $medium-gray: #cacaca;
56    $dark-gray: #8a8a8a;
57    $black: #0a0a0a;
58    $white: #fefefe;
```

Figure 6-10. Default secondary color

But in this example, we will be changing the secondary-color to lime. Open the _settings.scss file using Notepad++ or any text editor. In the Global section, change the secondary contextual color to lime. Refer Figure 6-11 to understand it better.

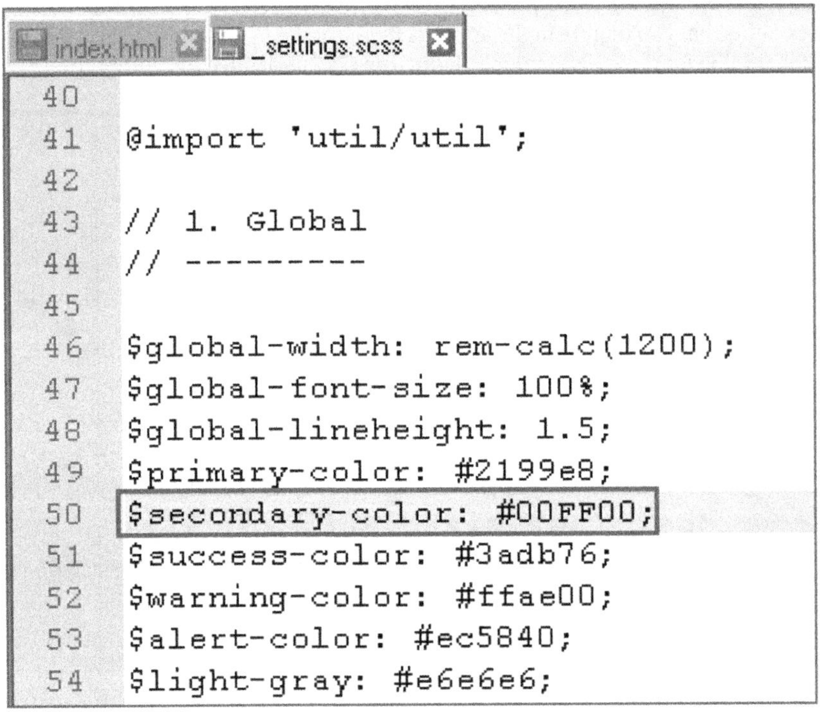

```
    index.html  ☒    _settings.scss  ☒
40
41  @import 'util/util';
42
43  // 1. Global
44  // --------
45
46  $global-width: rem-calc(1200);
47  $global-font-size: 100%;
48  $global-lineheight: 1.5;
49  $primary-color: #2199e8;
50  $secondary-color: #00FF00;
51  $success-color: #3adb76;
52  $warning-color: #ffae00;
53  $alert-color: #ec5840;
54  $light-gray: #e6e6e6;
```

Figure 6-11. Uncommenting and changing the primary color and font size

The Gulp Task runner will compile it automatically as displayed in Figure 6-12.

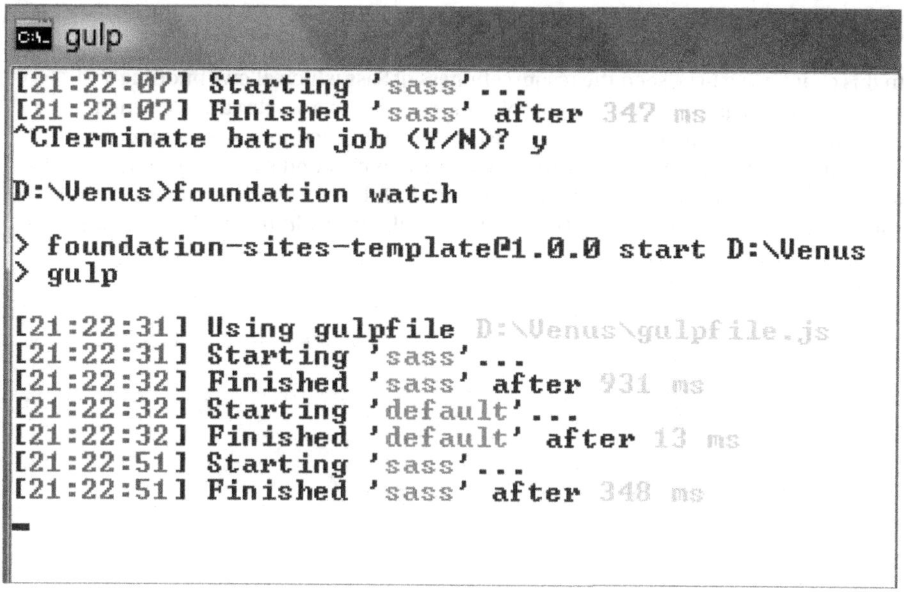

```
gulp
[21:22:07] Starting 'sass'...
[21:22:07] Finished 'sass' after 347 ms
^CTerminate batch job (Y/N)? y

D:\Venus>foundation watch

> foundation-sites-template@1.0.0 start D:\Venus
> gulp

[21:22:31] Using gulpfile D:\Venus\gulpfile.js
[21:22:31] Starting 'sass'...
[21:22:32] Finished 'sass' after 931 ms
[21:22:32] Starting 'default'...
[21:22:32] Finished 'default' after 13 ms
[21:22:51] Starting 'sass'...
[21:22:51] Finished 'sass' after 348 ms
```

Figure 6-12. *Automatic Compilation by Gulp*

Therefore, if you reload the webpage, you can see that the callout panel color changes to lime as changed in the Sass file. Refer the figure 6-13 to understand it better.

This is a secondary panel

Far far away, behind the word mountains, far from the countries Vokalia and Consonantia, there live the blind texts. Separated they live in Bookmarksgrove right at the coast of the Semantics, a large language ocean.

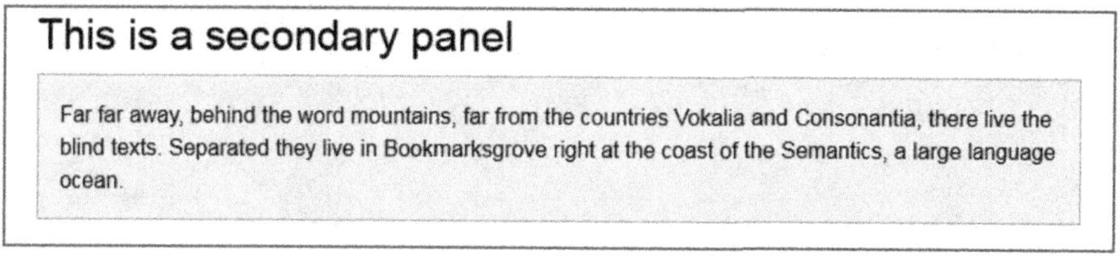

Figure 6-13. *Callout color changes to lime*

This is just the tip of the iceberg. Sass is an interesting pre-processor and is an ocean in itself. The more you learn, you will find that there is much more you can do.

For more info on just Sass, you can delve deep into many varied concepts and examples on the following link:

http://thesassway.com/

As for Gulp, you can always refer to the following link to understand it better:

http://gulpjs.com/

Summary

In this chapter, we have seen the resourcefulness of Sass which allows budding and experienced designers to abstract complex functions in to a single variable which otherwise would be quite cumbersome using CSS only. Therefore, with Foundation Sass, you can get your project up and running in a quicker and easier way. In the next chapter, we will take a look at the Foundation Hub where we learn about several community-related enhancements and built-in utilities in addition to the roadmap of this immersive and responsive framework.

CHAPTER 7

■ ■ ■

Foundation Hub

Foundation is a framework that is logically built with baked-in components that streamline the web-designing experience. The preceding chapters of this book were focused on Foundation for Sites. The present chapter touches on Foundation for Email, Foundation for Apps, and the extensive Foundation library of HTML templates and themes for incorporation in projects. The Foundation website contains a Building Blocks section featuring a pattern library of tailored HTML, CSS, and JavaScript snippets for use in Foundation web-designing projects. The present chapter shows you how to optimize your web design and leverage the benefits of using the ready-made Foundation resources at your disposal.

Foundation HTML Templates and Themes

The Foundation website contains an HTML Templates section where you can view several responsive templates tailor-made for different purposes. All of them are based on the Foundation Grid and cater to varied functionalities. For example, you have the Product Page, Agency, Blog w/sidebar, Blog Single Column, Ecommerce HomePage, and Portfolio templates (Figure 7-1).

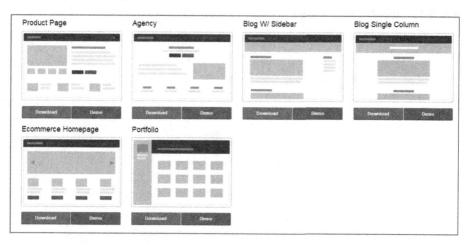

Figure 7-1. *HTML Templates.png*

Simply click on the Download button below the templates to download the webpage. You can also click the Demo button to display a preview of that webpage. You can find these templates at `http://foundation.zurb.com/templates.html`.

Building Blocks

Building Blocks are a pattern library for front-end components where you can find tailored code snippets to include in your Foundation Code. The Building Blocks can be found at `http://foundation.zurb.com/develop/building-blocks.html`(Figure 7-2).

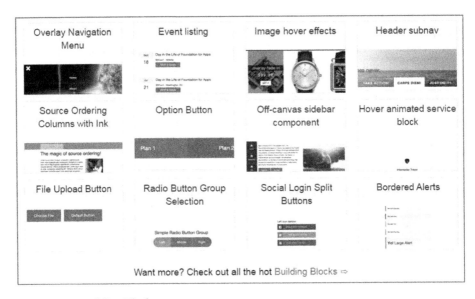

Figure 7-2. *Building Blocks.png*

You can check out all the Building Blocks at `http://zurb.com/building-blocks` (Figure 7-3).

Figure 7-3. *Sample Building Blocks*

It is so flexible that you can search the required pattern by clicking the Type link to view the different tags tailored for you to incorporate in your projects (Figure 7-4).

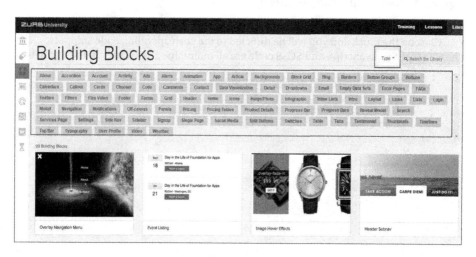

Figure 7-4. *Building Blocks filtered by Type*

Let's now look at the procedure to use the Social Login Split buttons building block (Figure 7-5).

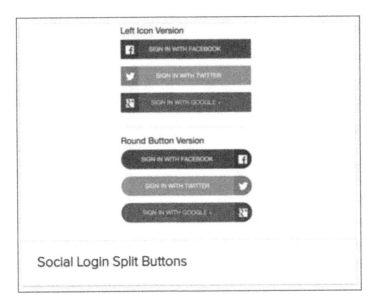

Figure 7-5. *Social media Buttons building block*

Click on the block and you will be directed to the corresponding code snippets. The HTML, CSS, JavaScript, and SCSS code are all maintained separately in their panels (Figure 7-6).

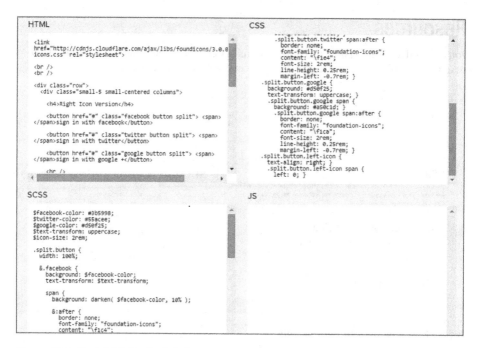

Figure 7-6. *Social Media Code Snippets*

Copy the code from their panels and paste it in your coding files. You can also change the content or customize the content or look according to your requirements.

Resources

You can find a library of add-ons and plug-ins at http://foundation.zurb.com/sites/ resources.html. Figure 7-7 shows a portion of the Resources page.

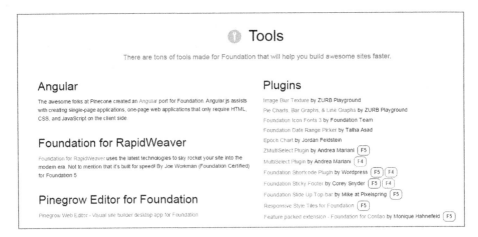

Figure 7-7. *Toolkits and Plug-ins.png*

In addition to many customizable toolkits and utilities, blocks for use in conjunction with frameworks such as Angular or Django are available here. Foundation Themes are not only tailor-made for content management systems (CMS) such as WordPress and Joomla, but also server-side systems such as .NET, Meteor, Python, and PHP.

Panini

The development team at Zurb created Panini to optimize prototype development. Inclusive of Handlebars and with Libsass baked-in, Panini encourages the use of templates, pages, and partials to speed up the prototyping process. It adheres to the DRY principle of "write once, use everywhere."Panini is a Gulp-powered build compiler tool that compiles Sass to CSS, helping you create HTML pages and reusable partials in flat files. You can also use it in conjunction with UnCSS to erase CSS classes and compress CSS, JavaScript, and Images.

Motion UI

Initially used in Foundation for Apps, Motion UI is available in Foundation for Sites in the Foundation 6.0 version. The Motion UI library aids in flexible transitions and animations for the UI. You can also create custom transitions other than the built-in CSS classes. Motion UI is versatile and flexible and may be used with any JavaScript animation utility.

Foundation Forums and Support

Foundation has lively community support and you can post queries on the Foundation Forums. You can also post your queries by email and on GitHub and Stack Overflow.

Zurb offers Foundation for Business as a premium support level for companies in development along with web-based and onsite training. The hosted code feature, Notable, allows s of project zip files to enable prototype presentations, prior to live implementation.

Foundation for Apps

Foundation for Apps is a power-packed framework that helps you build single-page web apps quickly. It can be used for developing apps for varied purposes such as email, chat, or travel portals. Combined with the power of AngularJS and Motion UI, you can create immersive apps with complex features quite easily. Since it utilizes AngularJS for implementing a MVC structure and UI Routing, the developers need not know AngularJS or JavaScript. For details, go to `http://foundation.zurb.com/apps.html`.

Foundation for Email enables device- and client-agnostic creation of responsive emails in conjunction with boilerplate templates and support for email clients such as Microsoft Outlook, Mozilla Thunderbird or Yahoo Mail. For details, go to `http://foundation.zurb.com/emails.html`.

Envoi

Coding gets better with practice. Play with the source code in the digital annex of this book, modifying it freely to gain a practical understanding of Foundation from the variations in output. The deeper you delve into the intricacies of Foundation, the greater will be your appreciation of its power. For ongoing updates and information, follow the Foundation blog at `http://foundation.zurb.com/learn/blog.html` and sign up for the Stay Connected Insider facility at `http://foundation.zurb.com/learn/foundation-insider.html`.

Index

Get the eBook for only $5!

Why limit yourself?

Now you can take the weightless companion with you wherever you go and access your content on your PC, phone, tablet, or reader.

Since you've purchased this print book, we're happy to offer you the eBook in all 3 formats for just $5.

Convenient and fully searchable, the PDF version enables you to easily find and copy code—or perform examples by quickly toggling between instructions and applications. The MOBI format is ideal for your Kindle, while the ePUB can be utilized on a variety of mobile devices.

To learn more, go to www.apress.com/companion or contact support@apress.com.